T0372338

Cambridge Elements ≡

Elements in Language Teaching
edited by
Heath Rose
University of Oxford
Jim McKinley
University College London

SOCIOCULTURAL THEORY AND SECOND LANGUAGE DEVELOPMENTAL EDUCATION

Matthew E. Poehner
The Pennsylvania State University

James P. Lantolf
*Beijing Language and Culture University
and The Pennsylvania State University*

CAMBRIDGE
UNIVERSITY PRESS

CAMBRIDGE
UNIVERSITY PRESS

Shaftesbury Road, Cambridge CB2 8EA, United Kingdom

One Liberty Plaza, 20th Floor, New York, NY 10006, USA

477 Williamstown Road, Port Melbourne, VIC 3207, Australia

314–321, 3rd Floor, Plot 3, Splendor Forum, Jasola District Centre,
New Delhi – 110025, India

103 Penang Road, #05–06/07, Visioncrest Commercial, Singapore 238467

Cambridge University Press is part of Cambridge University Press & Assessment,
a department of the University of Cambridge.

We share the University's mission to contribute to society through the pursuit of
education, learning and research at the highest international levels of excellence.

www.cambridge.org
Information on this title: www.cambridge.org/9781009507554

DOI: 10.1017/9781009189422

© Matthew E. Poehner and James P. Lantolf 2024

When citing this work, please include a reference to the DOI 10.1017/9781009189422

First published 2024

A catalogue record for this publication is available from the British Library.

ISBN 978-1-009-50755-4 Hardback
ISBN 978-1-009-18941-5 Paperback
ISSN 2632-4415 (online)
ISSN 2632-4407 (print)

Sociocultural Theory and Second Language Developmental Education

Elements in Language Teaching

DOI: 10.1017/9781009189422
First published online: May 2024

Matthew E. Poehner
The Pennsylvania State University

James P. Lantolf
Beijing Language and Culture University and The Pennsylvania State University

Author for correspondence: Matthew E. Poehner, mep158@psu.edu

Abstract: Sociocultural Theory (SCT), as formulated by Russian psychologist L. S. Vygotsky nearly a century ago, is distinct among traditions in the field of second language (L2) studies in its commitment to praxis. According to this view, theory and research provide the orienting basis for practice, which in turn serves as a testing ground for theory. This Element offers a synthesis of foundational concepts and principles of SCT and an overview of two important areas of praxis in L2 education: Concept-Based Language Instruction, which organizes language curricula around linguistic concepts, and Dynamic Assessment, a framework that integrates teaching and diagnosing learner L2 abilities. Leading approaches to L2 teacher education informed by SCT are also discussed. Examples from studies with L2 teachers and learners showcase praxis in action, and emerging questions and directions are considered.

Keywords: sociocultural theory, Dynamic Assessment, Concept-Based Language Instruction, L2 education, Vygotsky

ISBNs: 9781009507554 (HB), 9781009189415 (PB), 9781009189422 (OC)
ISSNs: 2632-4415 (online), 2632-4407 (print)

Contents

1 Introducing Sociocultural Theory

1.1 Introduction

The initial section provides an overview of the general theory as it was developed by L. S. Vygotsky in Russia roughly between 1924 and 1934 (the year of his early and untimely death at the age of thirty-eight). We explain the theory's foundational principles as well as the genetic research method Vygotsky proposed, which examines psychological processes and behaviors by tracing their origins and formation over time, including from present to future time, as happens during educational instruction. We then consider the implications of the genetic method for language education. In Sections 2 and 3, we discuss how the principles and genetic method are realized through particular educational activities. Section 2 discusses the pedagogical model referred to as Concept-Based Language Instruction (C-BLI) and includes examples from classroom research, while Section 3 addresses Dynamic Assessment (DA) along with some of the relevant research findings that have emerged from this approach to language assessment. In Section 4, we discuss two current models of teacher education that draw extensively from the theory. One model works with novice teachers at the university level and the other involves novice and in-service teachers who practice in primary and secondary schools. Finally, we offer some concluding remarks that summarize the discussion and consider implications of SCT–L2 for classroom practice.

1.2 The Historical Study of Consciousness

Sociocultural theory (SCT), or as it is also referred to, cultural–historical psychology, is a theory of the formation and functioning of uniquely human forms of mental behavior proposed by L. S. Vygotsky and his colleagues. In its theoretical and methodological perspectives, SCT assigns a central role to *history* as the process through which the human species, human cultures, and human individuals develop their abilities to learn, think, and act. As we proceed through our introduction, why and how history matters will become clear. The way to think about history in SCT is as change over time, but we must bear in mind that change is influenced by the purposeful activities of the individuals, communities, and species that are changed. Said in another way, humans change over time because we intentionally create the conditions in which change happens. This concept plays a central role in the educational process, which has as its goal the development, or change, of those who participate in the process.

To fully appreciate the importance of history in the formation of human thinking, what Vygotsky called the "genesis" of thinking, we need to discuss the new orientation that Vygotsky introduced into psychology. As with any scientific endeavor, the goal is to explain why any object, event, or system behaves as it does. To achieve this goal requires rigorous exploration of the reality of interest. This means that it is necessary to "look under the hood" to discover the factors that shape reality in specific ways, because those factors are often not open to direct observation by our senses, and in some cases our senses can lead us astray. For instance, our sense of sight tells us that the sun moves across the sky from morning to evening, and indeed many languages overtly express this misleading observation, as for instance when English speakers refer to the "sun rising in the East" and "setting in the West." For centuries this was the accepted belief because it was assumed that the Earth was the center of the universe and that the sun and planets revolved around it. It took a long time for science to discover and convince the general public that the universe is helio- rather than geo-centric. Indeed, if reality were in fact organized as it appears to our senses, science and education would be virtually unnecessary.

The general approach adopted in sciences such as physics, biology, and chemistry is to try to reduce an observed phenomenon to its elements, the smallest components that cannot be further reduced, on the assumption that these elements and interaction among them account for what we are able to observe. This idea can be traced back to ancient Greece, where it was believed that efforts to reduce matter would ultimately lead to their smallest, unobserv- able, basic components. These components were called atoms, or "uncuttable" elements. For a long time, it was believed that the atom was the smallest element of ordinary matter, but over time it was discovered that atoms are in fact comprised of even smaller elements – electrons, protons, and neutrons. Eventually, even smaller elements were proposed – quanta. The point is that a crucial procedure in scientific explanation is reduction, not for the sake of reduction per se, but because it is believed that all of material reality is likely to be comprised of a small set of elements. This approach has been carried over to the social and human sciences. Psychologists, for instance, sought to understand human behavior by reducing it to a small set of elements, called "reflexes," or reactions to environmental stimuli. One of the famous examples of this process that made its way into popular culture is Pavlov's salivating dog. This view held that living things, including humans, react to environmental stimuli in the same way that dogs in Pavlov's lab responded to the sound of a bell as a signal that they would be fed. In other words, behavior of all life forms, including humans, was reduced to reflexes that were either biologically inherited from ancestors or the result of conditional reactions to environmental stimuli.

Of course, plants and animals, including humans, do respond reflexively to environmental stimuli. Nonetheless, Vygotsky argued that following the reduc- tive procedure of the hard sciences would not be a productive way for psychology to understand human thinking. His proposal (Vygotsky, 1997b) was that psychology must identify the smallest *unit* (not element) that would allow us to observe and understand uniquely human forms of mental behavior. A unit should contain the basic features of the more complex object or process that we want to understand. He offered the following example to explain what he meant. If we want to understand the property of water that enables it to extinguish fire, we cannot reduce it to its elements, oxygen and hydrogen, because hydrogen is flammable and oxygen promotes combustion. Therefore, the smallest unit, given what we want to explain, is the combination of oxygen and hydrogen that is water. Transferring this idea to psychology, Vygotsky reasoned that there must be basic units that would allow us to study and understand human mental processes – processes that go beyond instincts and conditioned reactions to the environment. Among those basic units he included cultural concepts as they are represented in word meaning, which for him entails the unity of thinking and speaking (see Vygotsky, 1987).

Children are born with genetically transmitted psychological processes inherited from their ancestors. Thus, infants cry instinctively when they are hungry and they instinctively suckle when their cheeks are brushed by a nipple, or even a finger. This is not a behavior they learn. Adults also search for nourishment when they are hungry, as do all living things. However, unlike infants and animals, we can – up to a point – inhibit the search for food. Moreover, and unlike other animals, we can frequent special locations (i.e., restaurants) to satisfy hunger and we can even eat when we are not hungry simply to enjoy the pleasure of good-tasting food. Adults can also intentionally pay attention to certain events and objects and ignore others and we can choose to remember specific events and objects and ignore others. Unlike other species and children of our own species, we can imagine and think about realities beyond the immediate context in which we may find ourselves. We even have the capacity to design a way of achieving an imagined reality. What is it then about adult thinking that distinguishes it from children and that of other animals? There must be something that humans do not share with other animals and the young of our own species that makes the difference in thinking.

Vygotsky reasoned that humans (adults) must be simultaneously animals and not animals. We share natural instincts with animals but at the same time we have something unique that extends beyond instincts. He proposed that what makes us unique thinkers is human culture. While many have argued that other species of animals live in some configuration that resembles culture, the configuration is nowhere near as complex and as developed as human culture(s). Most importantly, there is one feature that human cultures have developed that animals and young children lack – the ability to speak. Speaking (we include sign language of Deaf communities, as well as writing or what Vygotsky called, written speech) is the key to the formation of human thinking, or what is called in SCT, *higher psychological functions*; that is consciousness. Our natural instincts and our learned reactions to environmental stimuli are more or less automatic responses to the world around us. If someone throws an object at us, we instinctively react to avoid being struck. If a particularly pleasurable or painful event frequently recurs, we learn to react positively or negatively to it. However, there are circumstances in which events in our world occur such that we do not have a ready-made way of reacting (instinctive or conditioned), yet we need to find some way of behaving that is appropriate for us. Consider a simple, but potentially fatal, circumstance in which a man finds himself in the woods confronted by a bear. His instinct most likely pushes him to turn and run. Yet, this could provoke the animal, which also reacts on instinct, to chase down its prey. Most of us would have little chance to outrun a bear. The man must inhibit his instinct to run away, not something that instinct prepares us to do, and must at the same time quickly devise a plan of action in order to survive. He might decide to freeze and not move and hope that the bear loses interest, or he might try to slowly back way while not looking the animal in the eye. This process requires a special kind of thinking that goes beyond instinct. The planning process is carried out through his higher psychological capacity, or consciousness – a process in which speaking to oneself is deeply implicated. The conscious mind imbues humans with a very powerful survival mechanism – the capacity to deal with unanticipated objects and events (Arievitch, 2017). Vygotsky (1993a, p. 57) acknowledged mind as "the most valuable biological adaptation" in all of nature, introducing "tremendous complexity" into human behavior "by giving it endlessly varied forms and by providing it with enormous flexibility."

In a very real sense, through the planning process we carry out an action mentally before executing it physically. Planning may be a simple process or it can be quite complex. Before constructing a building, architects work out complex plans using the support of artifacts such as computers to take account of all the factors that are necessary to construct the edifice (e.g., resistance against the forces of nature, including gravity). No worthy architect would consider constructing a building without a plan. On the other hand, deciding what to prepare for dinner requires a much less complex plan, but nevertheless, most of us do not just randomly throw ingredients together and hope for the best. We work out a plan in our conscious mind that takes account of our likes, dislikes, ingredients available, time, and so forth. What this means is that humans act twice before carrying out an action: once mentally and then materially. This includes not only constructing buildings and cooking meals, but also deciding how to interact communicatively with other people.

Vygotsky argued that psychology must answer the following questions: How is consciousness formed? How does it function in our life activity? How can its quality be enhanced? To begin to answer the questions, he proposed a set of principles as well as a new research methodology that has implications not only for general psychology but for education and for our purposes, language education.

1.3 Principles Guiding the Formation of Consciousness

1.3.1 First Principle: Mediation

Mediation: a "*transition from direct, innate, natural forms and methods of behavior to mediated, artificial mental functions that develop in the process of cultural development*" [italics in original] (Vygotsky, 1998, p. 168). This principle reflects "the historical development of human behavior" (p. 168) as cultures create different kinds of physical and symbolic tools to help them modify nature to survive and to improve their living conditions. For example, if we need to dig a hole to plant a tree, we can try using our hands as an animal might. However, it is much easier and more efficient to use a shovel – a cultural invention that enhances our ability to dig holes. If we need to plant many trees in a short period of time, we can use specially designed power machines – a more advanced version of hands/ arms and shovels. Similarly, if I want someone, such as a child, to move from one location to another, I can do so by physically pushing or pulling the person, or I can use another human creation – language – to achieve my goal symbolically. Both physical and symbolic tools, such as shovels and language are said to mediate human relationships to material reality and to each other. In other words, culturally created tools come between myself and reality (physical or social) and in so doing, change my relationship to this reality. For a fuller discussion of mediational tools, see Kozulin (2024).

1.3.2 Second Principle: Sociogenesis

Sociogenesis: "*the relation between higher mental functions was at one time a concrete relation between people; collective social forms of behavior in the process of development become a method of individual adaptations and forms of behavior and thinking of the personality*" [italics in original] (Vygotsky, 1998, p. 168). This principle captures the fact that every higher mental process appears twice in development, first interpersonally, between people, and then intrapersonally, within each individual. Thus, functions such as attention, perception, memory, imagination, emotions, logical thinking are in the beginning of our life mediated through our social relationships with other people. In early life, the other people are usually parents and older siblings. Later, as we grow, other individuals take on this role, including teachers, friends, co-workers, and so forth. How other people behave toward us and eventually how we behave toward them interpersonally affects how we relate to ourselves psychologically, or intrapersonally. This process takes place primarily through linguistic communication. A simple example having to do with perception should make things clearer. In early childhood, before we learn language, our natural perceptual instinct enables us to perceive objects and movements around us. However, prelinguistic children do not have any idea what they are perceiving until another person, such as a caregiver, tells them. Caregivers usually do not do this with a formal plan in mind, in the way a teacher might plan a lesson; nevertheless, it is through speaking with children that their natural ability to perceive is reshaped as a culturally constructed way to perceive. A child might see an object such as a drinking glass sitting on a table. The child has no way of knowing that the glass and the table are separate entities and might easily conclude that the glass is part of the table, until someone lifts and refers to the object as "glass" and also hears the other person refer to the object on which it was resting as "table." Over time, the child is likely to see "glass" in a variety of different contexts and will then come to understand that it is not a feature of table but is in fact a separate object, with a specific function.

As our language system develops, more and more parts of reality become visible to us as they are mediated through the meanings of our language, which is why words are important units of analysis for Vygotsky. Not only are we then able to talk about these parts, but we eventually are able to think about them as well. Thus, what was in the beginning perception mediated by others, interpersonally, becomes perception that is self-mediated, intrapersonally, but relying on the same symbolic meanings that others presented to us. Vocate (1994) described the shift from social communication between people to psychological communication within an individual as movement from "I ~ You" dialogues to "I ~ Me" dialogues.

Not only do we learn how to think about reality through mediation provided by others, we also learn how to feel as a consequence of "I ~ You" dialogues. We are born with a set of emotions that have developed over the course of human evolution. These include among others, *distress,* exhibited through crying as when an infant has an "urgent need" for food (Holodynski, 2013, p. 24) and *endogenous pleasure,* displayed through a smile and the relaxing of tension upon recognizing a caregiver's face (p. 25). During the enculturation process these natural emotions, also mediated by others, develop into more complex emotions as they are brought into language. Distress, for example, in Western cultures, morphs into frustration, anger, defiance, sorrow, and sadness (Holodynski, 2013, p. 26), while endogenous pleasure develops into pleasure, joy, affection, and amusement (p. 26). Just as with perception, once emotions are brought into language and become semantic emotions and not just biological feelings, we are able to understand what it is we feel as defined by our culture. Moreover, we can use language to talk about our emotions with others even if we do not experience them at the time. Indeed, before his untimely death, Vygotsky proposed a new unit of analysis for understanding consciousness – *perezhivanie* – the unity of intellect/cognition and emotion (see Vygotsky, 1994).

1.3.3 Third Principle: Internalization

Internalization: the "*transition of a function [is] from outside inward*" [italics in original] (Vygotsky, 1998, p. 170). The point of this principle, especially as it relates to principle 2, is that our psychological makeup is shaped by our social experiences. Thus, the connection between our psychology and our social world is necessary and inseparable. Humans as such are always social, even when alone because we always carry others with us in our I ~ Me dialogue what was originally I ~ You dialogue. Vygotsky (1997b, p. 170) stated this connection cogently and succinctly: "through others, we become ourselves."

The process alluded to in the third principle is described as *internalization*, which entails the use of language (i.e., speaking) to master, or regulate, our own mental and physical behavior. In so doing we gain freedom from coercion by the here and now of the immediate environment. Children are not able to understand and talk about the past and the future or about things not in their immediate surroundings until they have developed a sufficiently sophisticated language system that includes the means of talking and thinking about past and future objects and events – that is, things that are extra-contextual. This capacity is crucial in the development of free will, which Vygotsky (1997b, p. 171) equates with verbal behavior: "without speech, there is no will."

An important aspect of internalization is that it not only encompasses cognitive development but also entails the formation of culturally appropriate emotions that emerge from precursor natural emotions (i.e., distress, disgust, interest, startle, and pleasure) as mentioned in Section 1.3.2 (see Holodynski, 2013, pp. 24–25). As children are enculturated along with their cognitive development, their natural emotional instincts are linguistically restructured into a semanticized emotional system as they engage with members of their community. Thus, not only are they able to perceive natural objects as different as palms, pines, oak, and maples as belonging to the same superordinate category "tree," they are also able to perceive, think about, and linguistically express specific bodily reactions and feelings such as love, hate, anger, fear, shame, joy, and so forth, even when they are not actually experiencing these in real time. Concepts such as "tree," as argued by Danziger (1997), are not natural kinds, but are human kinds created throughout cultural history as communities interacted with nature. In other words, what is expressed through the English word *tree* is not a specific concrete object that would exist in nature in the absence of humans. What exist in nature are concrete objects referenced in English as palms, maples, pines, oaks, cypresses. Moreover, not all cultures have found it necessary to group the array of natural woody objects into a single category. Some indigenous communities in Australia do not have a word equivalent to English *tree*, but instead they have individual words for each of the wide variety of eucalyptuses growing in their environment. Similarly, semanticized emotions created from the precursor emotions are not universal across human cultures. For example, Ratner (1990, p. 78) points out that according to some anthropologists, indigenous North American Arctic communities lack the concept of "anger" "because they do not blame individuals for their actions," even though they may feel annoyed at a particular act perpetrated by someone else.

1.3.4 Fourth Principle: Developmental Stages

Developmental Stages: as every higher mental function is internalized it passes through four developmental stages (Vygotsky, 1997b, p. 103). The first is the stage where our natural innately specified instincts predominate. The second is the stage of external mediation of behavior by other people. It initiates the organization and subordination of the natural processes through social "I ~ You" communication. The third stage occurs when the individual begins to direct the symbolic means used by others toward the self in "I ~ Me" communication in order to mediate, or regulate, our own mental and physical behavior. This stage is associated with *egocentric* or *private speech* (Vygotsky,1987; Flavell, 1966) – speech that at first appears to be social in form but is psychological in function. The fourth stage appears when private speech is completely internalized and no longer overtly expressed. At this point, it becomes *inner speech*, which loses all the formal features of external speech but retains its meaning as it mediates our mental activity.

To give an example of private speech, consider someone trying to complete a jigsaw puzzle. As the person works on the puzzle, it would not be unusual for her to produce such utterances as "Now, the red one," or "Wait, wrong," "Blue."

As social speech, these utterances are difficult to understand, because they are not intended for an interlocutor. In other words, they are part of an "I ~ Me" dialogue in which the speaker directs (or mediates) herself through the difficulty of deciding which piece needs to be placed in a particular position. The speaker knows that "red" and "blue" refer to puzzle pieces of a particular color and she knows that "wrong" means something like "I made the wrong selection and I need to make a different one," but because she is engaged in a private dialogue it is not necessary to form a full utterance, as might happen in social speech. To be sure, social dialogues, given presuppositions that can be drawn on the basis of context and previous utterances, can take on an abbreviated appearance, also, as when two people are looking at a painting in a museum and one says to the other "beautiful." In the puzzle example, however, there is no interlocutor other than the self. Moreover, the motivation behind the puzzler's utterances is the problem of determining which is the appropriate piece to place in the puzzle at this point in the process. If there were no such problem, it is unlikely that she would produce such utterances and the task would be planned internally without any need to externalize the thinking process. The reason that the process is externalized is that when we encounter psychological difficulties, we tend to "reaccess" (Frawley & Lantolf, 1985) earlier stages of development, as stated in the four principles. The following quote from Vygotsky (1997c, p. 106) captures the essence of the theory:

> We might say that all higher functions were formed not in biology, not in the history of pure phylogenesis [evolutionary development of a species], but that the mechanism itself that is the basis of higher mental functions is a copy from the social. All higher mental functions are the essence of internalized relations of a social order, a basis for the social structure of the individual. Their composition, genetic structure, method of action—in a word, their entire nature—is social; even in being transformed into mental processes, they remain quasisocial.

1.4 Research Methodology

Vygotsky recognized that for any discipline to make progress in understanding and explaining its object of study, it had to formulate a research methodology that was appropriate for that object. He criticized psychology for borrowing methodology directly from the hard sciences in order to investigate the development and functioning of human mental processes. The problem Vygotsky recognized is that the world of objects such as planets, rock formations, atoms, electrons, gravitational and nuclear forces is very different from the human cultural world of symbols, meanings, social organizations, thinking, and emotion – a world where goals, motives, and images of possible futures predominate (Davydov interview in Levitin, 1982, p. 267). For this reason, Vygotsky insisted that psychology needed to produce its own methodology in conjunction with the principles of the theory (Vygotsky, 1997b).

Vygotsky understood that by limiting psychological research to the study of adult mental behavior under experimental laboratory conditions it would be virtually impossible to determine whether the behavior was governed by natural processes or cultural mediation. This is an essential question for psychology, especially given that SCT proposes that human mental behavior arose as a consequence of the restructuring of natural innate processes through culturally constructed forms of mediation. Here Vygotsky was critical of the methodology used by Pavlov in Russia and behaviorist psychologists in Anglo-American research. Measuring the reaction time of a participant in a controlled experiment, for example, is unable to determine whether the reaction results from instinct, conditioning, or from culturally mediated behavior. Vygotsky reasoned that the only way to disentangle things was to study the mind and its components (e.g., perception, attention, memory, emotion, imagination, creativity, and logical thinking) from a historical perspective. In other words, the processes entailed in conscious behavior must be investigated while they are being formed over time. Consequently, he focused much of his attention on the course of development as it occurred from childhood to adult life. Beginning from the assumption that as infants our mental behavior is subject to the natural processes we inherit from our ancestors and the learned behaviors we acquire through reactions to environmental stimuli, he reasoned that things would begin to change dramatically as soon as culture entered the picture, which begins during infancy as our caretakers interact with us in culturally specific ways.

An especially important factor in the cultural development of mental processes, as we have already discussed, occurs when language enters the picture around the age of two. Vygotsky's research showed, for instance, that when young children try to grab for a perceived object, parents frequently interpret this behavior as if it is a symbolic pointing gesture, which in fact it later becomes as the child, too, comes to recognize the meaning that the parents have imposed on the grabbing action (Vygotsky, 1997c, p. 104). This he interpreted as the beginning of symbolic interaction between parents and their children and a precursor to linguistically mediated behavior. As language develops over time, children become increasingly under the influence of their culture both in their physical as well as their mental behavior. A crucial point in the developmental process occurs when children begin to use language to formulate a mental plan prior to acting materially. For example, when asked to make a drawing, young children will often produce something and then decide what it is they produced. Thus, language plays a naming rather than a planning function. Eventually, when asked to draw, children will state what it is they intend to draw before drawing it. At this point, language exhibits a significant psychological function – a function that plays a key role in adult life.

The methodology that Vygotsky proposed in which the history of development is central he called "the genetic method." It is genetic, not in the biological sense, but because it is concerned with genesis, that is, "it introduces a historical viewpoint in the investigation of behavior" in order to trace the creation of the higher psychological system that is consciousness (Vygotsky, 1997b, p. 88). The genetic method is used not only to trace the formation of psychological functions from childhood to adulthood. It is also used to study the development of thinking in the life of communities as their cultural circumstances change. Luria (1976), a colleague of Vygotsky, investigated changes in the thinking of rural communities in the Union of Social Socialist Republics (USSR) when formal education and literacy were introduced in the 1930s. He discovered that education had a profound effect on how adult thinking changed as a result of schooling. For instance, when presented with a task asking which in a series of objects (e.g., dish, knife, fork, glass, eyeglasses) did not belong with the other objects, individuals who had not attended school indicated that all the objects belonged together, including the eyeglasses. They reasoned that without the eyeglasses it would be difficult to see the other objects, thus revealing a functional way of thinking. Those members of the community who had experienced even a few years of schooling ruled out eyeglasses, because they had learned a categorical or taxonomic way of thinking. Clearly, both ways of thinking are important depending on the activity one is involved in. However, schooling provided access to another way of mediating the thinking of members of the rural community.

In addition to using the genetic method to trace the development of consciousness across the life span as well as in cultural and societal changes, Vygotsky also brought the method into the experimental laboratory, referring to it variously as "an experimental-genetic method" (Vygotsky, 1997c, p. 68) or as "the instrumental method" (Vygotsky, 1997b, p. 88). In keeping with the goal of genetic methodology, the method uses artificial means to gain access to the process through which individuals develop the ability to integrate cultural forms of mediation into their mental behavior. The method also allows the researcher to access processes that may appear to be similar because they generate the same product but are in fact, from a developmental perspective, different. It seeks to reveal "real connections that are hidden behind the external manifestation of any process" (Vygotsky, 1997c, p. 69). The reasoning is that once a process has been completed and is functioning smoothly as often happens with adult thinking, it is difficult if not impossible to identify the source of the behavior. Thus, what appears to be the same behavior can have two different explanations, depending on its source. By the same token, two dissimilar behaviors can arise from the same source depending on the context in which the behavior occurs. Through the experimental-genetic method, Vygotsky attempted to resolve this problem.

Why does it matter that similar processes could arise from different sources and conversely, the same source could give rise to very different outcomes? It matters because unless we are able to probe beneath the surface of appearances, it is impossible to understand, explain, and potentially use or even change given aspects of reality, including ourselves. As we said earlier, appearances can be, and often are, deceiving. In many ways whales and fish superficially appear to be similar – living in water, feeding on similar food sources, and relying on similar forms of locomotion. However, probing these species more deeply, we discover that whales are air breathing mammals, while fish extract oxygen from the water through gills. Whales propel themselves through the water using flippers and their tail, which moves vertically, while fish propel themselves with fins and a tail that moves horizontally. Whales bear their young alive and suckle them until they are old enough to feed themselves, as with all mammals. Fish exhibit neither of these behaviors. To take another example, in the plant world we classify squash, corn, and tomatoes as vegetables; yet, botanically they are fruits and share more features with apples, oranges, and peaches than they do with lettuce, potatoes, and asparagus. In the domain of medicine, a cough can be a symptom of any one of a number of underlying problems. The task of a doctor is to discover which cause is the culprit in order to recommend appropriate treatment. Treating the symptom, the cough, is of little value and can have dangerous consequences, given that its cause could be a common cold virus, an allergy, or some life-threatening infection.

Vygotsky and his colleagues conducted a series of experiments following the genetic method with children and adults to determine how each group used their minds to solve problems. In one study, a memory task referred to as the forbidden color experiment, participants were asked to describe a variety of objects but were directed to not use the same color term more than once. In the first phase of the study, the children had a much more difficult time than the adults, frequently repeating a color despite the instruction. In the next phase, the participants were offered a set of colored cards with the suggestion that they might help improve performance. Neither the adults nor the younger children used the cards, while the older children figured that each time they mentioned a particular color they could set aside a card of that color as a reminder of its previous mention. In appearance, it looks as if the younger children and the adults failed to use mediation, while the older children did. The adults and the older children were successful in the task but the younger children were not. Upon further analysis the researchers showed that the adults, as with the older children, indeed had used mediation; however, it was internalized in the form of private speech. The adults were able to remind themselves verbally which colors they had already produced. Neither group of children had yet developed the ability for verbal self-mediation, but the older children understood that they could mediate their remembering through external means represented in the colored cards. Thus, comparing the adults to the younger children resulted in similar appearance in their behavior, although the children were inaccurate in performance. Comparing the adults to the older children, where the outward appearance of their behavior appeared to differ, in fact, in an import sense, it was not. Both performances were mediated, but in different ways. Using the experimental-genetic method, the study corroborated the theoretical principle that development moves from external to internal forms of mediation.

Finally, Vygotsky and Luria used the new method not only as a research tool, but as a means to improve the lives of individuals who suffered from various forms of deprivation or debilitation. Understanding that mediation is the key to higher forms of thinking, Vygotsky sought alternative forms of mediation for those who, for whatever reason, did not have optimal access to the mediational means provided by a culture. He showed special interest in blind and Deaf individuals as well as street children, who had been abandoned by their parents or those who had been turned over to orphanages where full access to language was often problematic. Luria (1973), for his part, worked with adults who had experienced brain damage due to stroke or other forms of injury. Some of these individuals had lost the capacity to produce connected speech – although they could repeat words and name individual objects. Luria asked a patient with the inability to produce connected speech when describing an event to write down on slips of paper in any order "fragments of the theme as they came into his head" (p. 322). The patient was then able to rearrange the fragments and "convert them into a coherent narrative" (ibid.). Luria thus relied on the principle of external mediation to overcome what was otherwise an impossible task to help the patient regain control over his mental behavior.

1.4.1 The Genetic Method and Education

Researchers in the hard and social sciences generally accept the segregation of theory/research from its practical applications whereby theory development and associated research are carried out independently and without regard for possible implications for making practical improvements in the life of a community. Accordingly, the goal of theory/research is to explain phenomena in any domain of reality that is hidden from observation. If the findings turn out to be practically relevant, so much the better, but if not, it does not matter. Vygotsky argued that there is no reason to segregate theory/research from practice in the social sciences in general, and in psychology in particular. For him, the ultimate arbiter of theory is not experimental research (although as we have discussed, it is important), it is practice, as he forcefully stated in the following quote:

> [in traditional psychology] Theory was in no way dependent on practice. Practice was the conclusion, the application, an excursion beyond the boundaries of science, an operation which lay outside science and came after science, which began after the scientific operation was considered completed. Success or failure had practically no effect on the fate of the theory. Now the situation is the opposite. Practice pervades the deepest foundations of the scientific operation and reforms it from beginning to end. Practice sets the tasks and serves as the supreme judge of theory, as its truth criterion. It dictates how to construct the concepts and how to formulate the laws. (Vygotsky, 1997b, pp. 305–306)

In the foregoing remarks, Vygotsky proposes a radical shift in how psychology should pursue research – one in which it can no longer segregate practical application of research from research itself. In other words, the application is not what we do after we have conducted research independent of practice; rather, practice itself is research – research that assesses the validity of the theory. Recall Luria's use of external mediation with the patient experiencing problems producing connected speech. Was he engaged in research or in clinical practice? Luria relied on the theoretical principle that this form of mediation is essential in the developmental process. If the patient had not responded favorably after writing down the unordered fragments relevant to the theme, it would have represented a significant challenge to the principle.

A practical domain that Vygotsky was intently interested in was education, which he considered to be not merely an activity concerned with knowledge acquisition, but in fact a crucial site for development of the person. As such, the principles of the theory are expected to operate as much in an educational environment as they do in everyday life but in a way that is distinct from everyday life. In other words, education involves a particular use of the instrumental method that intentionally and systematically brings to bear a form of mediation based on the conceptual knowledge that research in all domains, including the arts and humanities as well as the soft and hard sciences, has produced over the course of human history. This form of mediation Vygotsky called "scientific" or "theoretical" which he contrasts with "everyday" or "spontaneous" knowledge (Vygotsky, 1987). Scientific knowledge reveals aspects of reality hidden from direct observation through our senses. We have already mentioned several examples of scientific knowledge derived from research contrasted with everyday knowledge based on appearances (e.g., whales and fish; fruits and vegetables). Scientific knowledge not only allows us access to the hidden features of reality, it also provides vicarious access to human history (e.g., the French Revolution, feudalism, Roman empire, etc.) and to locations that most of us are unlikely to experience firsthand (e.g., Antarctica, deep sea, surface of the moon). Education accomplishes its task largely through systematically created, organized, and sequenced linguistic signs, "designed by an external agent," such as teachers, textbooks, syllabus, curriculum, and so forth (Wertsch, 2007, p. 185). Given its systematic, intentional, and explicit, focus, Vygotsky (1997b, p. 88) characterizes education as the "artificial development of the child," which "restructures all functions of behavior in a most essential manner." As students move through school, they not only acquire knowledge, which for Vygotsky is not the most important aspect of the educational process, but they enhance the "degree of mastery" (p. 88) they exhibit over their own behavior, which he regarded as the raison d'être of schooling.

1.4.2 Language Education

Over the years we have witnessed a swing of the pendulum in discussions of education, including language education, from so-called teacher-centered to learner-centered approaches. Currently, the pendulum seems to be stuck in the learner-centered position, where students are assumed to be, or at least encouraged to become, the agents of their own autonomous learning, usually in classrooms where explicit instruction, if it occurs at all, is relegated to a marginal role with implicit learning in various formats, such as VanPatten's model of processing instruction (VanPatten & Smith, 2022), or the Dynamic Usage-Based model proposed by Verspoor and Schmid (2024).

Education, including language education, has been influenced directly or indirectly by the writings of Swiss psychologist Jean Piaget, who proposed that development was governed by natural spontaneous processes which unfold in a specific sequence from simple, concrete, and empirical cognition to complex, abstract, and rational thinking (Wadsworth, 1984). Schooling then should take advantage of the assumed developmental sequence when it comes to organizing and implementing a curriculum in any subject matter. If instruction is not subordinated to natural processes, it will be ineffective and might even do harm to students. Consequently, students must be allowed to discover things on their own when they are ready and no amount of teaching can make a difference other than in trivial ways (Egan, 2002, p. 104). According to Egan (2002, p. 106), the problem with Piaget's model is that it focuses on responding to what students can do at any point in the educative process rather than on challenging them and helping them to pursue what they cannot yet do. A study by Kirschner, Sweller, and Clark (2006) analyzing research on different versions of discovery- and inquiry-based instruction (a legacy of the natural-child model of education) concluded that there is no significant evidence to support the approach, and that it may even have a negative impact "when students acquire misconceptions or incomplete or disorganized knowledge" (p. 84).

In language instruction, Piaget's ideas have at least indirectly influenced assumptions in the L2 field regarding so-called natural orders (Krashen, 1982), in which certain features of an L2 are predicted to be acquired before other features (e.g., English irregular past tense forms acquired before regular past tense forms) and developmental sequences (Pienemann, 1998), in which the acquisition of a specific structure such as negation or question formation in English unfolds in a specific sequence. Thus, in acquiring English negation learners are predicted to follow a predetermined sequence in which they first mark negation with "no/not" placed at the front of a sentence, as in "No John eat dinner"; later they insert "no" or "not" in front of the main verb, as in "John no/ not eat dinner" and both of these are prerequisite stages for the auxiliary "do" to appear, as in "John does not eat dinner."

On analogy with child language acquisition, the natural order and acquisition sequence hypotheses both presuppose that learner-internal mechanisms are responsible for guiding the L2 acquisition process whether it occurs in a natural immersion setting or in a formal classroom context (Long, 1997). Bearing this in mind, as with Piagetian educational theory, the claim is that instruction can only be effective if it is sensitive to those mechanisms that developmentally prepare learners to acquire the next feature in a natural order or the next stage in an acquisition sequence. Carrying through on this view, implicit instruction that provides a robust quantity of comprehensible exposure to a language should be more conducive to successful acquisition than is explicit instruction focused on specific features of the language. In other words, focus is on the learner and the learning process with the teacher having responsibility for providing learners with sufficient exposure to samples of the relevant features in natural comprehensible contexts that allow the internal mechanisms to operate.

The goal of implicit instruction, however, is based on two problematic assumptions: that so-called natural learning – how we learn outside of the tutored setting – is superior to well-organized intentional instruction (see Egan, 2002 for a detailed critique of natural learning in schools), and that the adult mind is not qualitatively different from the child mind. While adults might be capable of acquiring a new language through implicit processing in everyday immersion settings and through implicit forms of classroom instruction, the process is time consuming and often results in incomplete acquisition (Paradis, 2009, p. 118). There are a number of reasons that might account for incomplete acquisition: some features of the new language may not occur with sufficient frequency to allow learners to inductively figure out their meaning and how they function (e.g., some word-order options in Chinese); some features may be too subtle to detect in the high-speed world of day-to-day communication, even if they are frequently used (e.g., English articles); "attentional biases" emanating from a learner's L1 that can hinder the ability to notice L2 features (Ellis & Wulff, 2020); evidence from cognitive neuroscience research that the system responsible for implicit learning in childhood, procedural memory, declines as we age making it more likely that adults will increasingly rely on the system responsible for explicit learning, declarative memory (Paradis, 2009, p. 118). We return to this topic in our discussion of teacher education in Section 3.

SCT-informed language instruction takes a very different perspective in proposing that optimally effective pedagogy depends on well-organized systematic instruction that presents learners with conceptual knowledge of the language, especially of complex and subtle features that are difficult to appropriate from immersion context outside or inside classrooms. The knowledge must be made functional for communicative purposes, which requires not only practice opportunities but also effective mediation that guides learners as they undertake to gain control over and use the new language to create meaning.

1.5 Conclusion

In this section, we explained the four principles of SCT: mediation, sociogenesis, internalization, and developmental stages. The historically based genetic method was then discussed with specific consideration of its implications for language education. The remainder of this Element examines major lines of work in L2 education and teacher education informed by the theory. Paramount within the four-decade history of SCT-L2 research has been the shift from early uses of the theory as a lens for analyzing processes of L2 development to using the principles of the theory to diagnose and promote language development.

2 Concept-Based Language Instruction

2.1 Introduction

Sections 2 and 3 present two pedagogical models (one for instruction, the other for assessment) that integrate the four theoretical principles introduced in Section 1. Both models support the view that explicit instruction can be pedagogically effective if it is appropriately organized in accordance with the principles of the theory. In both cases, the key concept is that effective instruction leading to development depends crucially on interpsychological mediation, which occurs through engagement with teachers, assessors, classmates, and scientific concepts. The goal of the educational process, as indicated by the theoretical principles, is to promote the shift from interpsychological to intrapsychological functioning so that learners are eventually able to rely on their own abilities when engaging in communicative actions in a new language. In other words, learner autonomy is the goal rather than the starting point of education (Kozulin, 2024).

We first present the instructional model, as it has been adapted specifically for language instruction –C-BLI. We will then illustrate how the model has been implemented with examples from pedagogical studies, including the all-important materialization of conceptual information (explained in Section 2.2.3).

2.2 The Pedagogical Model

The original version of model, referred to as Systemic Theoretical Instruction, was formulated by P. Y. Gal'perin, a psychologist heavily influenced by Vygotsky's writings. Gal'perin's goal (see Engeness, 2021; Haenen, 1996) was to explain the process of internalization (i.e., movement from inter- to intra-psychological functioning) that occurs in the development of mental functions in any educational domain. He proposed a series of stages, or levels, that he argued promote the internalization process and with it the development of learners. We prefer to use "phase" rather than "stage" because in our view instruction designed to maximize learner development should be flexible and responsive to learner needs and instructional goals rather than implemented in a fixed sequence. Gal'perin, with his colleagues and students, conducted hundreds of pedagogical studies on the effects of the model on development in an array of school subjects, including foreign languages (see Haenen, 1996; Talyzina, 1981), although his approach to language analysis deviates from ours.

The modified model, which we call C-BLI, is presented in Table 1. As we work through the model, we will explain each phase and describe its contribution to the overall developmental process.

2.2.1 Phase 1: Pre-understanding

The Orienting Basis of Action (OBA) is the phase in which an action plan is formulated based on the current knowledge of students. The plan orients an action toward a specific goal and is "the most important aspect of the psychological

Table 1 Model of Concept-Based Language Instruction (C-BLI)

Phase	Description	Pedagogical rationale
1. Pre-understanding	Knowledge of concept prior to instruction – Orienting Basis of Action (OBA)	Identify and make visible starting point for instruction
2. Concept presentation	Coherent explanation of concept	Comparison between current and new knowledge
3. Materialization	Concretize (2) as drawing, graph, diagram, object as – Schema for the Orienting Basis of Action (SCOBA)	Avoid rote memorization. Holistic representation of concept. Easily remembered
4. Verbalize (languaging)	External speech/writing	Reveals understanding. Transform external to internal process. Shift from reliance on SCOBA to reliance on self.
a. Communicative	Explain concept and use to others	Speech to begin transformation process. Speech becomes psychological
b. Dialogic	Explain concept and use to self	Transform understanding to private speech
5. Performance	Use concept in goal-directed communicative activity	Ability to embed conceptual knowledge in purposeful practical activity
6. Internalization	Concept used without reliance on SCOBA or external speech	Concept generalizable and functionally useful

mechanism of an action" (Gal'perin, 1969, p. 251). Most of the time we act intentionally based on a plan that we formulate; we execute the plan and we monitor it to determine if the plan is adequately carried out or if it needs to be adjusted in some way. Keep in mind that a plan is a kind of action carried out mentally but not in reality. We can think of a plan as an instruction to ourselves to do something in a specific way. However, we can never know for sure how good the plan is until it is executed. Thus, there is a connection between planning, the focus of phases 1–3 and performing, phase 5.

Phase 1 is important because it informs the teacher and makes students aware of what they know or think they know about a language feature and how they use it to plan and carry out communicative action. Understanding what can be communicatively achieved (or not) through use of a feature of a new language is essential to the planning process. To be communicatively effective a language user must understand the expressive range that a language feature has the capacity to express. If learners' knowledge is limited, incomplete, or erroneous, their ability to effectively plan and execute communicative actions will be impeded. Problems with their knowledge can result from previous instruction where structure-based rules of thumb are presented. It may also occur through immersion experiences in which a feature is neither sufficiently frequent nor robustly salient, or if the feature was misinterpreted by a learner. The following is an example of a rule of thumb: use Spanish preterit whenever a past temporal adverb is used, as in *Ayer fui (preterit) al cine con mis amigos* "Yesterday, I went to the movies with my friends." While the rule is appropriate for the particular context, it does not reflect the option of using imperfect aspect with the same temporal adverb, as in *Ayer el presidente hablaba (imperfect) con los líderes europeos* "Yesterday, the president spoke/was speaking with the European leaders."

2.2.2 Phase 2: Concept Presentation

Coherent explanation of a concept so that learners can understand it and when possible, compare it to their pre-understanding revealed in phase 1. The concept must focus on the meaning of each feature rather than its structure. Of course, the structure matters, but C-BLI finds its inspiration in research that has been carried out in meaning-based, rather than structure-based, theories of language – in particular, Cognitive and Systemic Functional Linguistics (CL or SFL). While we find inspiration in these theories, for pedagogical purposes, it is at times useful to modify details of the theoretical explanations to ensure learner understanding. To appreciate the relevance of meaning-based language analysis, we will offer an example borrowed from Langacker (2008).

According to Langacker (2008, p. 43), meaning is comprised of content and the specific way a user construes, or chooses to view or perceive, the content. A glass containing water is observed by different speakers of English. One speaker may be motivated to attend to, or construe, the object as "the glass of water." Another speaker may be motivated to construe the content of the glass and decide to express this as "the water in the glass." Two other speakers might attend to the quantity of water in the glass. However, in this case, there might be a difference in their construal of the quantity. One might see the glass as "half empty" and the other as "half full" (Langacker, 2008, p. 44). Speakers express, or profile, their construals through different linguistic means. This informs a listener of the particular aspect of the object that a speaker has in focus, which in turn influences how a listener might construe the object. The teacher's task is to impart to students the ways in which a language enables speakers to profile their particular construal of objects, events, and states.

We can also construe events in a variety of ways. For instance, consider a simple event such as the following: *person(X)/action (left)/object (her lunch)/ location (at home)/frequency (for the third time this week)*. A speaker might construe this event in a variety of ways, such as a more or less neutral way without highlighting any particular component of the event: "Sally left her lunch at home for the third time this week." However, a speaker might construe the frequency component of the event as salient, in which case she might profile that component by positioning its representation at the front of the utterance, as in "For the third time this week, Sally left her lunch at home." Another speaker might construe the object and profile it by positioning its representation at the front of the utterance as in "Her lunch, Sally left *it* at home for the third time this week." Notice that in English, when a speaker profiles an object, it often entails use of what is called a resumptive pronoun (e.g., it). This can occur in response to a question such as "What happened to Sally's lunch?" It would, however, be an odd response to the question "What happened?" In this case an appropriate response would be "Sally left her lunch at home for the third time this week." Finally, a speaker might choose to construe Sally as the salient component of the event, in which case she would be profiled as in "Sally, *she* left her lunch at home for the third time this week." This utterance would not be an appropriate response to the question "What happened?" Also notice use of the resumptive pronoun "she." The meaning of the utterance is quite different from an utterance that does not profile Sally (example borrowed from Langacker, 2008).

The process that profiles a constituent of an utterance, as in the examples in the preceding paragraph, is referred to as "topicalization." It has the effect of indicating that the profiled constituent is the topic of the utterance – what the utterance is about. In the preceding examples, we saw that it could be *how frequently* Sally left her lunch at home; or *the object* that Sally left at home, or even *who* left her lunch at home. Languages can topicalize constituents in a variety of ways, but word order is a frequent way of doing it. As we will see when we discuss phase 3, a language such as Chinese profiles a topic in some ways similar to, but in some ways different from, English.

To summarize: phase 2 is the point at which a language concept is systematically presented to students. The teacher needs to be sure that the explanation is understood by students. However, it is important that the goal is not for students to memorize the explanation but to understand it. In fact, in phase 3 the concept is presented to students in a nonverbal visual way, which, if prepared appropriately, will avoid the tendency to memorize without understanding.

2.2.3 Phase 3: Materialization

In this phase the teacher presents students with a visual representation of the concept explained in phase 2. This representation is known as a Schema for the Orienting Basis of Action (SCOBA), or Schema for the OBA. Recall that orientation is central to the planning process. It is the point at which a person surveys a situation, determines, if and how to (re)act, assesses the resources available to (re)act and then develops a plan of action. SCOBAs represent the linguistic resources (conceptual knowledge) available for communicative action. They represent the resources in a holistic external form. Recall that development is understood as a process whose source is found in socially organized relationships and/or culturally created artifacts. SCOBAs are intended as a way of complying with this principle. Because they are visual, as well as tactile (see Figure 1), SCOBAs are crucially holistic, something that is difficult to achieve in verbal explanations. If prepared properly, SCOBAs avoid the tendency of students to memorize, often without understanding, as often happens with verbally presented definitions and explanations.

In a study on teaching Chinese topicalization reported in Zhang and Lantolf (2015), the instructor used two different SCOBAs to visualize the concept for his students. One was a power point animation depicting someone who ate a bowl of rice at home at a specific time of day. The animation showed how to profile the adverbs of time and place as well as the object (bowl of rice) by placing them in the appropriate topic position. In addition, the instructor also used a tactile SCOBA, illustrated in Figure 1, that enabled the students to manipulate the topicalization process with their hands. Depicted in the figure are Cuisenaire rods, often used in teaching math and associated with the Silent Way methodology (Gattegno, 1972).

The students manipulated the rods in order to demonstrate the various options for profiling different constituents in Chinese utterances. The verb in Chinese cannot occupy any other position, which is indicated by the size of the rod – the verb cannot move. Nevertheless, it is possible to profile a verb in Chinese utterances, but how this is done is beyond the scope of our present discussion.

The study challenged the teachability hypothesis, which claims that learners follow a specific sequence when acquiring certain features of a new language, such as the formation of English negative constructions (Pienemann, 1989). For Chinese, the hypothesis asserts that topicalization occurs in three stages. The first is the normal canonical S (Adv) (Adv) V O order, "The man at 2pm at home ate a bowl of rice." The second is the ability to topicalize adverbs, Adv S (Adv) V O, as shown in Figure 1: "At 2pm the man at home ate a bowl of rice," or "At home the man at 2pm ate a bowl of rice." The third involves positioning the object in topic position O S (Adv) (Adv) V, "A bowl of rice, the man at 2pm at home ate." According to the hypothesis, acquisition proceeds through three stages: 1>2>3. Stages cannot be skipped; thus, even under instruction 1>3>2 is not possible and stages 2 and 3 cannot be acquired at the same time. Nonetheless, Zhang and Lantolf (2015) reported that through C-BLI students could develop the capacity to spontaneously use stage 3 before stage 2 and that it was even possible to develop the ability to use both stages simultaneously (see also Zhang, 2020). The point is not that C-BLI is some kind of magic bullet but that mechanisms of development are not contained within the individual; rather, they are situated between the individual and the social environment, which if appropriately organized can affect developmental processes.

A particularly interesting outcome of the Chinese study is the performance of one of the students, who was assessed as having a low level of working memory (WM), the mental system that "keeps things in mind while performing complex tasks such as reasoning, comprehension and learning" (Baddeley, 2010, p. 136). On narrative and interview tasks that assessed the learners' ability to topicalize

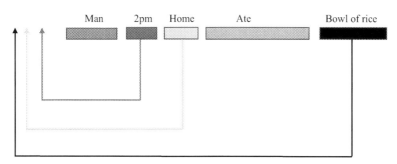

Figure 1 Tactile SCOBA for Chinese topicalization

appropriately in spontaneous speech, the student performed as well as students with normal and high WM. When this student spoke in Chinese, however, she moved her hands as if she were manipulating the Cuisenaire rods, even though the rods were not physically present (Lantolf & Zhang, 2017). This is not a surprising outcome, given the mediational principles considered in Section 1. Indeed, as Egan (2002) points out, while our hands are not part of our brain, they indeed can function as part of our mind. The study provided additional evidence that external forms of mediation, if appropriately organized, can enhance the developmental process.

A more recent study (Kissling, 2023) on C-BLI and Spanish verbal aspect provides further evidence that this approach to explicit instruction can significantly alter the anticipated course of L2 development that is assumed to depend on learner-internal mechanisms. Andersen (1991) proposed the Aspect Hypothesis (AH), which claims that all L2 learners will adhere to a specific predictable sequence when acquiring languages that morphologically mark aspectual differences. Spanish is one of those languages as it formally marks the distinction between perfective and imperfective aspect. According to the AH, learners will first mark perfective and imperfective aspect that matches the lexical aspect of a verb. Without getting into details (see Kissling for fuller explanation), verbs such as jump, throw, and hit indicate actions that are inherently bounded, in which the action occurs instantaneously (see in Section 2.3.2 for a SCOBA illustrating this language feature). When someone throws an object such as a ball, as soon as the ball is released the action is completed. Verbs such as talk, walk, write are inherently unbounded, whereby the action does not imply a clear end point. A third category of verbs describes states, such as like, be, and know, which are inherently unbounded. Thus, the AH predicts that learners will first inflect Spanish verbs according to their inherent lexical aspect: Bounded verbs with preterit and unbounded verbs with imperfect and that only later will they learn to inflect unbounded verbs for perfective and bounded verbs for imperfect aspect, in what is called viewpoint aspect. Kissling reports that following C-BLI absolute beginners, produced appropriate viewpoint aspect without first marking lexical aspect, in contradiction to the AH, when completing oral narrative posttest and delayed posttest tasks. Indeed, their performance, especially on the delayed posttest, was closer to native speakers and advanced L2 speakers than is documented for beginning and intermediate learners in the Spanish Learner Language Oral Corpora project. To quote Kissling (2023), C-BLI "helps novice Spanish L2 learners avoid relying on lexical aspect (aspect inherent in verbs and predicates) to motivate their uses of Spanish preterit (PRET) and imperfect (IMP), as the AH predicts they will do in the early stages of learning."

2.2.4 Phase 4: Languaging

Verbalization reflects the importance of speaking in the mediation of mental activity (see Section 1). We adopt the term, *languaging*, as suggested by Swain (2006), to capture the process of psychological speech, to distinguish this use of language from verbalization intended to socially communicate with an interlocutor. The significance of languaging is that students begin to relate to their speaking as a teacher relates to it and it produces a self-awareness of what they (think) they know and of what they are doing (Gal'perin, 1968, p. 260). Languaging, as a psychological process, begins to move students away from reliance on the external SCOBA and toward reliance on themselves when carrying out an action. Speaking, of any kind, has both a material aspect (sounds, or in the case of writing, marks on a page) and a symbolic aspect. The material side makes it observable and the symbolic side allows us to abstract away from a particular context or object, such as a SCOBA, and in a sense take it with us. It is interesting that the student in the Chinese topicalization study used part of her body, which of course is material, to symbolically replace the rods in the SCOBA – she had virtually transported the SCOBA with her.

There are two subphases of phase 4 that contribute to the abstraction process necessary for internalization. Making one's understanding and use of a concept comprehensible to someone else relies on the important connection between social and psychological function of speech. Explaining to another enables the other to understand but at the same time it helps the speaker understand something more deeply. Moreover, it is important for teachers to access students' knowledge of a concept and how they deploy it in communicative activity in phase 5. This subphase is called communicative languaging. The dialogic phase transitions to self-talk, which over time becomes increasingly abbreviated as in the puzzle example presented in Section 1, and is important because it entails the ability to control our mental activity through speech even when someone else is not there to listen. At first the speech is external but eventually, in phase 6, it transforms into inner speech and will no longer be overtly observable.

The first example of languaging is from a student struggling to reconcile what he had previously been taught about Spanish verbal aspect and the new knowledge presented in Negueruela's class. At the midpoint in the semester, through communicative languaging, the student revealed his problem: "It's more difficult to speak and rationalize using a certain tense for me, mainly because the reasoning is different from what I've been taught in the past. I'm still stuck trying to rationalize it using old methods and it gets confusing sometimes" (Negueruela, 2003, p. 356).

26 *Language Teaching*

The student's confusion created by the clash of old and new knowledge is an important component of the developmental process. Later in the semester, the student seems to have resolved the conflict when commenting on the new conceptual knowledge:

> it's a more abstract way of thinking about it, so instead of saying 'ok, this situation uses this particular rule, so I need to use this tense' I say 'what is the point I'm trying to express here, and which tense best accomplishes that.' I think I've learned how to effectively communicate my ideas better. I need to consider the aspect that I wish to emphasize and what the meaning is behind the words that I'm saying so that the verb tense helps people understand what I'm saying as much as the actual verb I use. (Negueruela, 2003, p. 253)

When students experience conflicts in their thinking, teachers can play an important role in helping to mediate and resolve the conflict. For Vygotsky (1987), conflict, which he described as a drama is an important source of development. Without the clash of current and future (new) knowledge there is no motivation for change. However, unless the conflict is made overt, it is unlikely that teachers will even be aware of what is going on. Languaging plays a key function in exposing and resolving the drama. In Section 3, we address ways of mediating students when they experience difficulties using new concepts.

How students react to the languaging phase is also revealing particularly since psychologically oriented speech is not something students have likely experienced through other pedagogical models. One student from Negueruela's class remarked that "Although sometimes recording myself speak was a bit awkward, I think it was overall extremely helpful. It made me more comfortable speaking and improvising, and it forced me to truly think about the grammar." (Negueruela, 2003, p. 308). Another student said, "I feel as though with verbalization exercises I not only improved my speaking, but also learned a lot of information about the indicative and subjunctive" (Negueruela, 2003, p. 308).

In a C-BLI study by Yáñez-Prieto (2014) with a more advanced Spanish class, students explained through languaging why they made specific aspect choices when creating personal narratives. Following a presentation on Spanish verbal aspect, including a sequence of SCOBAs (available in the article), the students created a written story on a topic of their choice. They were then asked to explain how they decided to manipulate aspect to create certain temporal perspectives in the story. One student offered the following set of comments:

> In my third draft I use the present in the bar and I use the imperfect to unfold the story as it happens in the past. I wanted to keep the suspense so I used the imperfect. Each event unfolded like walking around the corner . . . you don't know what to expect next.

> The things that can be done with words is [sic are] amazing. There's almost a magical aspect to it. They [sic] way words can inspire visions in the head is an amazing feat.
>
> Language is so amazing and can be used in so many ways to mean so many things. It can be manipulated into beautiful stories and suspenseful novels.
>
> I think writing is an art. The words are my paint. (Yáñez-Prieto, 2014, p. 198)

The student's comments show a deep understanding of how language can be used creatively to profile events in different ways just as an artist might visually manipulate reality to impart particular impressions on an observer. Clearly, this requires understanding of the concept of aspect well beyond how it is traditionally explained in textbooks through rules of thumb. It is worth noting that the student's comment is not restricted to Spanish but references "language," an indication perhaps that she has developed a deeper appreciation of how to create in her native language.

It may seem to some teachers, as Gal'perin (1968, p. 259) points out, that engaging students in languaging activity is "an encumbrance in class work." However, the pedagogical research that he and his colleagues (see Talyzina, 1981) carried out in nearly 800 schools showed that omitting this phase of the model markedly slowed down the developmental process resulting in greater difficulty for students to achieve control over a concept (Gal'perin, 1968, p. 259). Languaging is essential for shifting from the social to the psychological function of language. It empowers the individual to engage in abstract reasoning as it mitigates the need to rely on objects, such as SCOBAs, to mediate thinking. The ability to reason about one's behavior, as illustrated in the above languaging excerpts, is essential for full development.

2.2.5 Phase 5: Performance

The performance phase is open to the preferences of teachers, students, and programmatic policy. The essential point, however, is that without linking conceptual knowledge to concrete goal-directed activity, education falls victim to intellectualism. Vygotsky (1987, p. 169) stressed that everyday knowledge lacks the capacity for abstraction, meaning that what we appropriate in everyday life is not always open to consciousness and therefore not subject to voluntary control and generalization. On the other hand, he also cautioned, if scientific knowledge developed in school is not sufficiently saturated with concrete activity, the result is "*verbalism*" [italics in original] (p. 169), or "the mindless learning of words" (p. 170) in which the concept itself is missing. Holzman (2009, p. 48) captures the importance of saturating knowledge with concrete activity in the distinction she makes between schooling as "acquisitional" or as "developmental" learning. In the former, schooling produces "knowers," while in the latter it produces "learners," by which she means students come to understand that learning is what people do. It is not what people know.

While we recognize that the pedagogical activities such as task-based learning and content-based instruction can be ways of saturating knowledge with concrete action, we believe that drama-based approaches to teaching are especially appropriate for a pedagogical model grounded in Vygotsky's psychological theory. As we mentioned, drama played a central role in Vygotsky's thinking about development, most especially when he referenced the work of the great director, actor, and theatrical teacher, Stanislavski as contributing to his thinking about human development in and out of school. In theatrical drama there is a "collision of characters on the stage" (Veresov, 2010, p. 88), something Vygotsky transferred to what he saw as happening between individuals in the social drama of real life. Veresov provides the example of a debate between two people to illustrate what Vygotsky may have had in mind in conceptualizing development as drama. In a debate the participants generally adopt and argue for opposing viewpoints on an issue. This, Veresov speculates, could result in the participants reflecting on what transpired after the debate is concluded. Perhaps one participant may think that she made a mistake on a particular point during the debate or perhaps she expressed herself in an overly aggressive way. The reflection entails several mental processes: memory of what happened, emotion at having said something wrong and in an inappropriate way, volition, and determining that future behavior must change (p. 88). Consequently, the person changes and in the future behaves in a different way. This is development. In his analysis of development from infancy to adolescence, Vygotsky (1998) stressed the dramatic collision, or crisis, between children and the specific social reality that surrounds them at each age and how the resolution of the collision results in a transformation, or development of the children. A critical aspect of the collisions is emotional reaction of the individual. Indeed, Vygotsky (1994) criticized contemporary psychology for ignoring the intimate interconnection between emotion and thinking. For him, emotion provided the motivation for thinking (and speaking).

During the performance phase, especially early on, students might need to rely on phase 3 SCOBAs to help support their use of a language concept. However, as they gain experience manipulating a particular concept or set of concepts, they are expected to decrease their reliance on the overt manifestation of SCOBAs. As this happens, it is an indication that they are transitioning to internalization – phase 6.

Strategic Interaction

One way to introduce drama into phase 5 is through the approach to language instruction proposed by Di Pietro (1987). The approach creates dramatic tension between interlocutors through what is called a scenario. In a scenario, unlike in typical role plays, interlocutors are presented with a situation in which each has a vested interest in the interaction and its outcome, but each is unaware of the interest of the other person. At the initial stages of language study, once a role has been assigned, students work in groups to formulate a possible script that an interlocutor might produce to advance her position, all the while not knowing what another group is formulating for the second interlocutor. As each role is being prepared the teacher provides students with appropriate language as requested. This might include vocabulary, grammar, pragmatics, and discourse. Of course, the concepts that have been addressed in the course should also be included as appropriate. Once each group has settled on their script, they select a representative to play their respective role. They also help the actor rehearse the script. The actors are then brought on stage to carry out the interaction. The dramatic tension is generated by each actor not knowing the motive of the other. As in real life, it is necessary for the actors to figure this out as they engage with each other. If it turns out that a planned script is not working once the interaction is underway, students can ad lib if they have the ability and proficiency to do so, or, especially for less proficient students they can be given some time to return to their respective groups to revise the script before continuing the interaction.

It is best to video record scenario performances for analysis. It is important to not only pay attention to the verbal language, but also to the body language, including gestures, facial expressions, and emotion, which is analyzed in the debriefing phase of the process. During debriefing the teacher and students comment on all aspects of the performance, including its nonverbal aspects.

One of the difficulties that learners at all levels of verbal proficiency have when using a new language is their ability to display and communicate appropriate nonverbal features. Especially important in this regard is the expression of emotion, which entails not only knowledge of appropriate linguistic expressions of emotion, but also tone of voice, intonation, volume, eye gaze, proxemics, and haptic manifestations (i.e., is one allowed to touch an interlocutor, or is it taboo etc.?). The expression of emotion is not given sufficient attention in language classrooms; yet, as Vygotsky (1987) stresses, it is central to human psychological behavior. In fact, he argued that it forms a unity with intellectual behavior, providing the motive for action, physical as well as mental and verbal (see Dewaele & Moxsom-Turnbull, 2020). This explains Vygotsky's proposal of a new unit of analysis – *perezhivanie* (see Section 1). Once a scenario has been played out and analyzed, students should have the opportunity to create alternative outcomes. The scenario can then be reenacted by different interlocutors. The new scenario can be debriefed and analyzed and compared to the first enactment for language, strategies used by the interlocutors, authenticity of each performance, the emotional components of each, and so forth.

The following is an example of a scenario developed by van Compernolle (2014) in his study on three features of French interpersonal pragmatics, *tu ~ vous; on ~ nous; ne . . . pas ~ pas*. In this case, the students prepared their scripts individually rather than in groups and therefore decided on their own how they wished to play their role and present themselves socially to an interlocutor, played by the instructor.

Role A: You must return a defective toaster to the department store. Unfortunately, you have lost the purchase receipt and you have only your lunch hour to take care of the matter. Prepare yourself for an encounter with the salesclerk.

Role B: You are a salesclerk in the hardware department of a large store. You have been ordered to be careful in accepting returns of merchandise that may not have been purchased at the store. Prepare yourself to deal with someone who is approaching you with a toaster.

An especially rich source of scenarios can be also found in literary works, plays, and news items about events in real life. The latter provides students with opportunities to develop their creative abilities as they formulate possible roles based on the description of the events. Di Pietro (1987) points out that by using literary passages in particular students can have the opportunity to carry out written analyses of the original scene as created by the author and the scenario derived from it as enacted by the students.

A student from Negueruela's Spanish class offered an insightful comment on the experience of scenarios:

> I feel the most beneficial activities were when we improvised in class with a partner. We always wanted to do our best because it was recorded, so it forced us to use all Spanish, and it allowed us to think on our feet, and to really learn how to have an actual conversation. Yes, we messed up a lot, and we had to think about what we were going to say, leaving large pauses in the conversations, but it gave us practice for the future, when we actually are using Spanish. (Negueruela, 2003, p. 256)

Improvisation

Perhaps a more demanding way of introducing drama in phase 5 activities is through improvisation, which is not easy to carry out, even in one's native language. It takes practice and patience, but the rewards can be many. According to Holzman (2009), improvisational drama is a powerful means of promoting development. The term itself means "without preparation" or "spontaneous" and is a way of dealing with "the unexpected" (p. 61). Improvisation is a process that appears in many different everyday venues, spanning the world of business to the world of creative arts (e.g., music, dance, and acting). For Holzman, the value of improvisation is that it opens a place where individuals can become other than what they already are. They can experience feelings, emotions, and ways of thinking and behaving that they may have not experienced before.

Improv, according to Holzman (2009, p. 61) "is a performance art in which an ensemble of actors creates scenes or stories without a script." The actors work "off each other to create the stage, characters and plot—to go anywhere and make anything happen" (p. 61). It combines elements of "pretend play, game play and theatrical play to create something other than any of them" (pp. 61–62). There are two foundational rules of improv that all actors must agree to follow; if not, the entire process will collapse: *accept offers and build with them and don't negate* [italics in original] (p. 62). Offers are anything that an actor does or says from a verbal comment to a facial expression, a physical gesture, a grunt, a cough, a puff of air emitted from the lips, or doing nothing at all. The acceptance of an offer can be exhibited in an array of ways, but it must be accepted and not negated. If one player says, "I think I saw you last night at the opera" and the other responds with "Really, you should have said hello. We could have had a drink during the intermission." An offer is made and accepted. However, if the interlocutor responds with "It couldn't have been me, I wasn't at the opera last night." The offer is negated, and it becomes more difficult for the interaction to progress.

Improvisation is closely connected with play in childhood. Vygotsky argued that in play children have the opportunity to perform above their current ability (Vygotsky, 1978), such as when they pretend they are mommy, daddy, an astronaut, or a superhero. In play the rules are usually tacitly understood, unlike in game playing where the rules are explicitly stated and where violations destroy the game. This can happen in children's play as well, if a child fails to behave the way that an astronaut, mommy or daddy, or a superhero is expected to behave. Often the child is called out at that point as not playing appropriately. Through improv adults have an opportunity to "rediscover the creative and collaborative skills they had as children" (Holzman, 2009, p. 64).

To our knowledge, no one has attempted to implement improvisational drama in a C-BLI classroom. Given the preceding discussion, this seems to be an approach with much potential to impact development, and we hope that it will be explored by teachers in the future. It will be particularly interesting to monitor the emotional components of the interactions and to debrief students on their feelings and attitudes toward the process itself. For possible ideas on implementing improvisational activities, we recommend Lobman and Lundquist (2007) on improv in education. Although its focus is on elementary school, it does offer some ideas that could be adapted for secondary and postsecondary education. A more theoretical series of discussions of drama and improv in education can be found in Davis et al., (2015).

2.2.6 Phase 6: Internalization

In this phase, learners have internalized a concept and no longer need to rely on mediation from a SCOBA, a teacher, or anyone else to support their performance. The individual can access the concept with sufficient speed, although not necessarily as fast as a native user, to participate in spontaneous communicative interactions and/or to produce meaningful written texts. We comment on speed of performance in Section 4. This phase emerges as a result of the activities carried out in phase 5. As learners engage in additional, and more complex, activities they come to rely on themselves as autonomous self-mediated performers and are able to create meanings that reflect their own expressive and communicative goals. This is the phase of *inner speech*, where planning what to say (or write) is carried out covertly in the individual's mind before it is executed overtly.

2.3 Examples of Phase 3 SCOBAs

In this section, we present additional examples of SCOBAs that have been implemented in recent C-BLI studies. There is no right or wrong way to formulate a SCOBA. The goal of the instructor should be to find an effective way to make conceptual knowledge visible, understandable, and useable by students in a particular educational context, depending on such factors as age, experience, and students' language background.

2.3.1 English Particle Verbs

A feature of English that is often difficult for learners to master is the category "particle verbs," comprised of a verb core followed by a particle such as in, on, over, up, down, and so forth. Examples of such verbs include "run over," "look up," "let down," "make up," and "single out." The difficulty learners encounter with particle verbs is their metaphorical use, such as in the sentence "The football team *let down* their fans by losing the long-awaited match with their

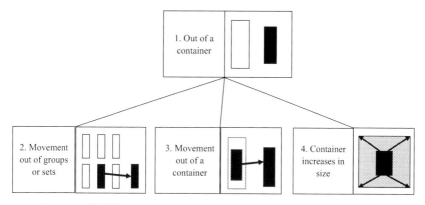

Figure 2 SCOBA for verbal particle *out* (Lantolf & Poehner, 2014)

cross-town rivals." Traditionally particle verbs are presented to students as lists that they memorize without much understanding of how to interpret their metaphorical meaning. However, using the concept-based approach of cognitive linguistics, a C-BLI study by Lee (2012) and reported on in Lantolf and Poehner (2014) formulated an effective way to explain and visually represent the meaning of particle verbs. The crucial aspect of the explanation is for students to understand that the metaphorical meaning of these verbs is derived from their literal meaning. The SCOBA presented in Figure 2 captures the relationship between the literal and figurative meanings of verbs formed with the particle "out."

The eight sentences below exemplify the various meanings of particles verbs with "out." The numbers in parentheses indicate which of the four options applies to the sentence.

1. I sleep with my hands *out* of the blanket. (1)
2. The man *went out* of his mind with anger. (3)
3. The large dog *ran out* of the pack and attacked the stranger. (2)
4. The professor *singled out* the new theory for special attention. (2)
5. The dog *jumped out* of the window. (3)
6. How did the police *figure out* who the criminal was? (2)
7. The caterers *spread out* the food across the table. (4)
8. I *filled out* my tax forms incorrectly. (4)

2.3.2 Spanish Verbal Aspect

One of the most difficult problems for English speakers to master in a romance language such as Spanish, is verbal aspect when it is expressed in the past tense. Aspect is a temporal perspective to profile events and states. It is a common, if

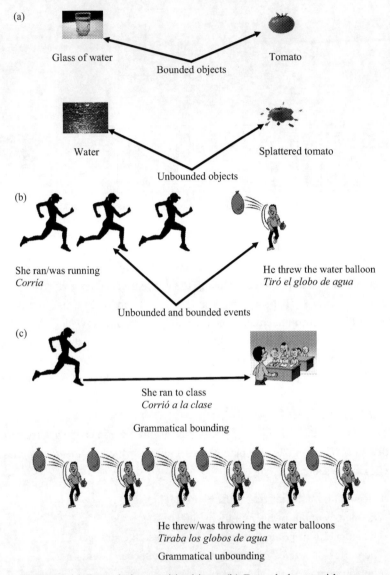

Figure 3 (a) Boundedness with objects (b) Boundedness with events
(c) Grammatical Boundedness

not universal feature, of language. Many languages indicate a wide array of
verbal aspects, including English. The problem that English-speaking learners
of Spanish face is that in the past tense, a Spanish speaker has the option of
marking a past event using either of two verbal aspects – preterit or imperfect.
English speakers certainly can construe past events from a different aspectual
perspective, but the language does not have clear options, such as specific verb
endings, for profiling the distinction.

Briefly, the underlying feature that captures the aspectual distinction is "bound-edness." This is a feature not only of language but also of objects in the world. For instance, water is by its nature unbounded because it does not have a specific recognizable shape. Its shape is determined by the container in which it is put, such as a lake, a glass, a pool, an ocean, a puddle, and so forth. Other objects are naturally bounded in that they have clear limits that we can observe, such as a ball, a fork, an apple, a piece of cake. Events are also naturally bounded or unbounded. The action of "walking" is temporally unbounded because in theory and with sufficient energy one could walk without end. Other events such as jumping, or throwing a ball, are temporally bounded in that they have temporal limits – a natural beginning and a natural end. When someone jumps the event begins and there is a natural end as the person returns to the original position or achieves some other end point, as jumping down the stairs. Grammar, however, allows a speaker or writer to profile what is naturally a bounded event as unbounded and vice versa, an unbounded event as bounded (see viewpoint aspect discussed in Section 2.2.3). The SCOBA in Figure 3 represents the conceptual notion of boundedness. To profile an event as unbounded Spanish speakers use one set of verb endings and to profile an event as bounded they use a different set of endings. Kissling and Muthusamy (2022) created animated SCOBAs for Spanish aspect available on YouTube.

2.4 Conclusion

C-BLI brings the four theoretical principles discussed in major Section 1 into concrete educational practice with the goal of promoting the development of learner ability to use the L2 autonomously to create and express their own meanings. The instructional process begins with the externalization of prior understanding learners may have of the language feature that is to be internal-ized. It is important for teachers, and learners, to recognize the starting point of the developmental process and to compare this with the new knowledge to be presented. Generally, L2 learners' prior understanding is based on structural rules of thumb rather than conceptual knowledge that foregrounds meaning. The sociogenetic process is mediated both by the teacher and by the SCOBAs that schematize the knowledge to be internalized. Languaging serves two functions: it informs the teacher of learner understanding of the new knowledge and it also promotes the internalization of that knowledge. In order to gain control of language concepts, learners must be given ample opportunity to use the concepts in spoken and written communicative activities. Although a variety of activities can be deployed to engage learners, we find particular value in those that are based on drama, especially improv, because such activities provide ample opportunities for learners to be creative and imaginative in their performance. While learners at first may have to rely on external mediation provided by the teacher and the SCOBAs, with extended performance opportunities their need for external forms of mediation is expected to decline as they internalize conceptual knowledge and use it autonomously and spontaneously. Thus, in C-BLI learners move through the developmental phases of the internalization process from external teacher- and SCOBA-based mediation to autonomous self-based mediation. For an overview of C-BLI studies reported in the literature, see Lantolf and Beckett (2009); Lantolf, Xi, and Minakova (2021).

3 Dynamic Assessment

3.1 Introduction

Recall that the first of Vygotsky's four theoretical principles is mediation, which is central to his approach to explaining the formation of consciousness as well as to researching developmental processes. The goal of Section 3 is to argue for the importance of mediation as a component of language assessment that first identifies learner abilities that have already developed (ripened, using Vygotsky's metaphor) as well as those that are in the process of developing (the buds and flowers, as Vygotsky put it) and to further promote their development. The principle invoked during assessment is to offer mediation when learners begin to struggle and their performance breaks down. At that point, mediation should be relatively implicit, and may include encouragement to try again or a general reminder of what the task requires. More explicit forms of mediation are offered only if needed by learners as they work through the assessment. In this way, the use of mediation in assessment differs from the explicit introduction of concepts that occurs in C-BLI. The reason for this is that while C-BLI aims to guide learners toward developing new ways of understanding and ultimately using language, mediation during assessment seeks foremost to probe learner abilities that are in the process of ripening. If only explicit mediation were offered during an assessment, the opportunity to determine how a learner might have responded to less implicit mediation would be lost, and with it the full picture of a learner's development. This way of carrying out assessment is generally referred to as Dynamic Assessment or DA.

We begin with a brief illustration of how DA might unfold with L2 learners. We then trace the origins of DA to Vygotsky's discussion of the Zone of Proximal Development (ZPD). Major approaches and formats that have been formulated by DA researchers, both within the L2 field and in general education and psychology, are introduced. This is followed by examples of some of the procedures through which DA has been implemented in L2 contexts.

3.2 Illustration of DA with L2 Learners

Poehner and van Compernolle (2020) reported using a DA procedure with US undergraduate university learners of L2 French. Its goal was to understand learner difficulties with various features of French grammar as they transitioned from basic to more advanced language courses. The tasks followed an elicited imitation procedure in which learners listened to a sentence in the target language and then had to repeat what they heard and explain in English what the sentence meant (see Section 2 for a discussion of why explanation is important). Each sentence contained the relevant grammatical constructions, and in some cases they were formulated incorrectly in order to determine whether learners noted the mistakes. As one example, the sentence *Ma soeur Jeanne lentement n'a bu *pas son café aujourd'hui* "My sister Jeanne didn't drink her coffee slowly today" was presented. In addition to the compound verbal tense construction (*a bu*), it also contained the negative particles *ne* and *pas* as well as the adverbial *lentement*. Errors occurred with each of these components; in its corrected form, the sentence would be *Ma soeur Jeanne n'a pas lentement bu son café aujourd'hui*. We consider two examples from Poehner and van Compernolle (2020) that contrast how learners respond to such sentences.

The two excerpts involve one-to-one interactions between the mediator and Nicole and Chris (both pseudonyms). We focus on the mediation provided as the learners work to understand the meaning of the sentence and to correct its errors as well as how responsive both are during the procedure. This information sheds light on their understanding of these features of French grammar, in particular, how near they are to controlling such constructions independently.

In Excerpt 1, Nicole has correctly interpreted the sentence's meaning ("My sister Jeanne didn't drink her coffee slowly today") without any difficulty. In line 1, she realizes that there is an issue with the word order.

Excerpt 1

1.	Nicole:	so it should be *n'a lentement* (pause) mm
2.	Mediator:	if you have a negation and an adverb, what do you do?
3.	Nicole:	(pause) um *n'a pas lentement*? mm *bu*?
4.	Mediator:	mhm, yeah *n'a pas lentement bu.*
5.	Nicole:	okay.
6.	Mediator:	so listen again, and tell what's wrong here. (plays audio)
7.	Nicole:	it said *lentement n'a pas bu*? instead of *n'a pas lentement bu.*
8.	Mediator:	okay.

Nicole required minimal support from the mediator to produce the appropriate construction. Independently, she correctly positions the adverb *lentement*, she also inserts the negative particle *n'* in the appropriate position. She mistakenly omits *pas*, but she corrects this as well after the mediator's question concerning negation and adverbs (line 2). In the final portion of this exchange, the mediator plays the sentence again and Nicole repeats it with its errors as well as the corrected form. According to Poehner and van Compernolle (2020), Nicole required minimal mediation throughout the DA session, although she was unable to complete the tasks entirely independently. This suggests that while her understanding of the complex syntax involved in compound tense constructions that include negatives and adverbs was advanced, it was not yet fully developed. From the perspective of the ZPD, Nicole would likely develop these abilities without much additional instruction and practice. Thus, we observe evidence of the buds or perhaps flowers but not yet the fruits of development.

Chris's interaction with the mediator in Excerpt 2 offers a useful point of comparison. He was initially confused by several elements in the sentence, including the name (*Jeanne* or Jane), and the mediator played the sentence a second time. At this point, Chris correctly interprets *ma soeur Jeanne* to be my sister Jane and then moves to the rest of the sentence. In line 3, he produces the compound verbal construction with the adverb *lentement* but using the affirmative rather than the negative form.

Excerpt 2

1.	Chris:	oh my sister Jane?
2.	Mediator:	mhm,
3.	Chris:	um *lentement* again, it should be *a lentement bu sa café? ce matin?*
4.	Mediator:	mhm
5.	Chris:	oh so my sister Jane uh slowly drank her coffee this morning.
6.	Mediator:	okay is it is it my sister Jeanne slowly drank her coffee?

The mediator accepts the affirmative construction from Chris, who then renders it into English. In line 6, the mediator repeats Chris's translation with a questioning intonation, presumably to determine whether he realizes that the French sentence actually expressed that Jeanne did not drink her coffee slowly. Chris confirms that he believes this is correct, and after some additional discussion, the mediator invites Chris to listen to the recording a third time and offers the further prompt to confirm whether the sentence is in fact in the affirmative.

7.	Mediator:	listen to it one more time and see if it's um affirmative or negative (replays audio)
8.	Chris:	oh it's negative it's (inaudible)
9.	Mediator:	so
10.	Chris:	*n'a bu pas? sa café aujourd'hui* right so
11.	Mediator:	where does the where does *pas* go?
12.	Chris:	*n'a pas?* i- it it I think it came after *lentement* but it should go *n'a pas lentement* right? or di- drank her coffee slowly today.

13. Mediator: so how would it be in French?
14. Chris: *Ma soeur Jeanne* uh *n'a pas lentement bu sa café aujourd'hui.*
15. Mediator: there you go okay.

Chris continued to struggle even after recognizing that it was a negative construction he was hearing. He required additional prompts in line 11, as the mediator draws his attention to the placement of the particle *pas*, and again in line 13. However, Chris's correct insertion of *ne* and *pas* in line 12 reveals his understanding of how to form negative constructions, and after only being asked to put all the elements together, does he produce the correct utterance in line 14. In comparison with Nicole, Chris required more extensive mediation to arrive at an appropriate performance. Nonetheless, another interesting outcome of the DA procedure reported by Poehner and van Compernolle (2020) is that while Nicole consistently required minimal support over the course of the assessment, the mediation that Chris needed steadily decreased from task to task. In effect, Chris appeared to close the gap with Nicole. The point is that the learners began in quite different places and followed contrasting developmental trajectories, information that would have been obscured if the procedure had targeted only their independent performance (van Compernolle & Poehner, 2020). The mediating process portrayed in the excerpts and the insights they yielded into the learners' development are important to keep in mind as we consider the theoretical framework behind DA.

3.3 DA Principles, Formats, and Approaches

3.3.1 Theoretical Basis for DA: The Zone of Proximal Development

The preceding example showed how important information about learner abilities can be revealed when assessments depart from the typical procedure of observing individuals as they independently complete tasks. This innovation in assessment began with two important observations Vygotsky (2011) reported from his work with children. The first was that some children identified as having special needs and placed in remedial programs responded well to instruction frequently closing the gap with their age peers. This meant that an individual's performance in school could be changed if appropriate forms of instruction were available. The second observation occurred in his examination of children's performance on standard tests such as IQ administered upon entering school. He noted that children with initially high scores performed well in school but when retested later some had not improved their scores and that among students who began with lower scores, some performed better at the end of the school year. Vygotsky's interpretation of this was that the school curriculum provided the challenge necessary for some learners to develop but not others.

Consequently, Vygotsky (2011) argued that all students would be better served if they were grouped so that instruction aligned with abilities that were maturing rather than those that had already matured. He reasoned, however, that a different kind of assessment was needed: "it is common to think that an independent solution of the problem, without any help, points to the level of the development of intelligence . . . [but] what is indicative of the child's intellectual development is not only what he [sic] can do himself, but probably more so what he can do with the help of others" (Vygotsky, 2011, p. 203) .

Vygotsky then reported piloting-mediated assessment by contrasting two ten-year-old children, both of whom were only able to independently complete tasks designed for eight-year olds. When the children were offered mediation such as reminders, leading questions, a demonstration of principles involved, hints, and feedback, important differences appeared: one child managed to complete tasks at the level of a nine-year-old and the other a twelve-year old. The point was not that the children did better when offered mediation, but that the extent of their improvement was not the same (Vygotsky, 2011). Their independent performance did not predict how they would respond to instructional support, and it is this responsiveness that is most relevant to future development.

Vygotsky formalized this research in his discussion of the ZPD. The ZPD refers to those abilities that have not yet matured but are still maturing. In most assessments, learners are required to operate without support, and so they rely exclusively on abilities that have already developed. What is revealed by such assessments is the learner's past; that is, development that has occurred up to the time of the assessment. This, Vygotsky (1998) insisted, is only part of the picture. In fact, he regarded the ZPD as more important for education because effective teaching should target abilities that are emerging rather than those that have already completed their developmental trajectory. It was for this reason that identifying a learner's ZPD is of "great practical significance" for education (Vygotsky 1998, p. 204). Therefore, assessment must be broadened to encompass both the past and future of development as accomplished through learner independent performance on assessment tasks but also how they respond to mediation.

3.3.2 Sandwich and Cake Formats of DA

Vygotsky's colleague, A. R. Luria (1961), first shared research on the innovative approach to assessment with an international community of psychologists and educators. The term "dynamic" to describe assessment that captures the ZPD seemingly originated with Luria's presentation, and soon afterward researchers began to design their own approaches to DA. Given that each approach developed in a specific cultural context, for use with particular learner populations and focused on a distinct set of abilities, differences exist among the approaches. Each is characterized, however, by the inclusion of mediation during the DA procedure as well as analysis of learner responsiveness as part of the diagnosis of their abilities.

Sternberg and Grigorenko (2002) coined the terms "sandwich" and "cake" to designate when mediation is offered, with the most popular format following a three-step process: (1) learners complete the assessment independently; (2) the assessor and learner review the assessment together, with the assessor offering mediation to probe learner understanding of problem areas; and (3) the learner independently completes a parallel version of the original assessment. The three steps together constitute the DA, with the mediation "sandwiched" between two traditional assessments. This format may seem familiar as it resembles the pretest – intervention – posttest design frequently employed in experimental research. As with such research, the sandwich format enables comparisons of learner performance prior to, and following, mediation.

Budoff (1968) and Budoff & Friedman (1964) carried out early sandwich-based DAs. At the time, US racial minority children were referred for special education services in schools at much higher rates than their majority peers. The researchers used a sandwich format in tests of general cognitive ability, reasoning that learner responsiveness to mediation could indicate the extent to which they would need special education support before rejoining their peers. They reported that it was possible to distinguish learners whose initial score was very high, those who evidence substantial improvement on the retest, learners who made modest gains, and those who failed to improve. Some DA researchers, beginning with Budoff, have employed the term "learning potential" to express the degree of change in learner performance through mediation, suggesting that high learning potential indicates relatively little instruction will be needed before a learner is able to independently reach the level of performance currently accessible with mediation only. Such information offers one way of capturing the ZPD of individual learners and may be used to inform instruction and other decisions about learners (e.g., program acceptance or placement at an appropriate level of study).

The "cake" format involves a single assessment administration. Mediation is provided following each assessment item or task, thus creating layers similar to the layers of a cake. An advantage of this approach relative to the *sandwich* format is time efficiency. In addition, Reuven Feuerstein, a leading DA advocate, argued that for learners with a history of academic struggle, excluding an independent pretest avoids reinforcing negative experiences (Feuerstein, Rand, & Hoffman, 1979). Feuerstein originally formulated his DA model with children who had survived the Holocaust and were relocated to Israel. He refined it through decades of clinical work with children facing extreme developmental difficulties, many of whom could not have their needs met in local schools. Excluding a measure of independent performance means that the cake format does not permit pre- and post-mediation comparisons. Instead, attention is given to the amount and quality of mediation as well as to learner success in identifying and overcoming their mistakes.

3.3.3 Interventionist and Interactionist Approaches to DA

Just as the timing of mediation varies in DA, so too does the quality of mediation available to learners. DA generally begins with implicit and shifts to more explicit mediation depending upon learner responsiveness. The logic here is that if a learner is offered an explicit form of mediation, such as stating the nature of the problem and the principle to be followed to overcome it, we have sacrificed the nuance of the diagnosis, that is, the ability to differentiate among learners according to their ZPD. In fact, if obtaining insights into a learner's ZPD is not the goal, then we could simply correct their errors, as some SLA researchers have suggested, and not engage in mediation at all. However, this would mean, for instance, that the L2 learners such as Nicole and Chris, might be regarded as having reached the same developmental level because neither learner succeeded in completing the assessment task independently.

Although all DA approaches organize mediation from implicit to explicit, some standardize mediation in advance of procedures, while others favor an open-ended approach in which mediation emerges through dialogue with learners. Lantolf and Poehner (2004) label these *interventionist* and *interactionist* approaches, respectively. In *interventionist* DA, each mediating "move" is arranged as a protocol or script that is followed in precisely the same manner with every individual. Standardizing the procedure facilitates interpretation of assessment outcomes, whereby it can be reported that one learner required two mediation moves, while another needed four to complete the same task. This can also be formalized in how scores are reported in *interventionist* DA. For example, scores can be adjusted to award points according to the quantity of mediation a learner requires such that a learner who completed an assessment task worth five points receives three points if two mediation moves were needed, while a learner needing four moves would receive one point.

Advocates of *interactionist* DA worry that following a script might miss important diagnostic information. In *interactionist* DA, the assessor is free to ask questions that probe learner understanding even when a correct response is submitted. The assessor can also offer various forms of support when errors occur and may introduce hypotheticals beyond the current task to verify learner reasoning. Such mediation is difficult to quantify; therefore, outcomes of these procedures are frequently reported in the form of qualitative profiles of learner performance and the mediation employed. While profiles do not allow for comparisons the way scores do, they do offer in-depth information to guide instructional decisions. For this reason, *interactionist* DA lends itself particularly well to classrooms, tutoring, and clinical contexts where the focus is on obtaining as much information as possible into learner abilities. *Interventionist* DA, on the other hand, is especially well-suited to more formal assessment situations where priority is given to generating scores.

3.3.4 Reciprocity, Transcendence, and Transfer

If mediation draws our attention to what the assessor does, the other side of that coin is what the learner does. While some researchers use "responsiveness" to describe learner reactions to mediation, others prefer the term *learner reciprocity*, coined by Lidz (1991, p. 10), which encompasses more than correcting mistakes. Lidz discovered that children engaged in behaviors that could be usefully included in diagnoses of development but that went beyond whether they improved their assessment performance as a result of mediation. Van der Aalsvoort and Lidz (2002, p. 122) subsequently proposed eight categories of learner reciprocating behaviors: responsiveness during interaction with the mediator; self-regulation of attention and impulses; affective quality of interaction with the mediator; communication related to shared activity; comprehension of activity demands; use of mediator as a resource; reaction to challenge; and modifiability in response to interaction. The researchers note that there may not be relevant observations in each of these categories, but they encourage practitioners to consider these and perhaps other forms of learner engagement in their diagnoses. For example, a learner who has difficulty regulating impulses may resort to guessing, which complicates interpretations of their performance because it can be difficult to distinguish errors that result from guesses and those that reflect reasoning problems. Similarly, through attention to learner communication during the activity, it is possible to ascertain how they perceive the task and the process through which they arrive at their response. These aspects of learner engagement might become targets for instructional intervention.

Transcendence and *transfer* are related but not identical concepts emphasizing that the focus of DA must always be learner development and not merely successful task completion. DA should not be considered a form of "training" to help learners become more efficient at completing a particular task. Instead, DA seeks to understand the abilities that learners draw upon as they complete tasks, where they experience difficulties, and the quality of effort needed to promote their development. The abilities in question, while invoked by the assessment task, are not limited to it but should apply to other situations learners are likely to encounter in the future. The term *transcendence* was introduced by Feuerstein (Feuerstein, Feuerstein, & Falik, 2015) to express this idea. For Feuerstein, memorizing the answer to a multiplication problem allows learners to correctly answer that problem, but learning how to multiply numbers prepares learners for any such problem they may face because these abilities *transcend* the immediate task.

Transfer formalizes this reasoning into DA by including tasks that depart from those learners have previously encountered, introducing new parameters or degrees of complexity. Campione et al., (1984) and Brown and Ferrara (1985) pioneered the use of transfer tasks in their DA research involving children's literacy and numeracy development. The aim of Brown and Ferrara's (1985) approach is to generate two axes of learner abilities, one representing how quickly learners grasp new principles and concepts and the other capturing how well they apply those when facing novel situations. To this end, learners first complete *near transfer* problems that are similar to tasks they have previously worked through with mediation but that require use of the concepts they have learned in new combinations. For *far transfer* problems, learners need to use similar but slightly different concepts in addition to those they have already learned in order to reach the solution. Finally, *very far transfer* problems are even more complex and may push learners to use concepts in novel domains. While the details of how *transfer* is used may differ from one study to another, the principle that we should be able to recontextualize our abilities is in line with Vygotsky's view of development. Indeed, for instruction to promote development, learners need to continue to be challenged by tasks that push them to extend their development to new and more complex domains.

3.4 L2 DA

Using DA in L2 contexts began in the early 2000s (e.g., Antón, 2003; Kozulin & Garb, 2002; Lantolf & Poehner, 2004). Some of the initial examinations of L2 DA were concerned with understanding mediation and learner reciprocity, and so they were conducted in tutoring settings in which one mediator interacted with one learner. We discuss three of these projects (Ableeva, 2010; Poehner, 2005, 2009) as they have had a substantial influence on subsequent L2 DA studies.

3.4.1 Processes of Mediation and Learner Reciprocity in L2 DA

Poehner (2005) implemented DA with university intermediate-level learners of L2 French that focused on their conceptual understanding and use of the tense–aspect system. Students completed oral narration tasks in which they watched brief videos and then recounted what occurred using French. The mediator used an interactionist cake format that probed the learner's knowledge of French tense and aspect, specifically *passé composé* and *imparfait*, including their reasons for selecting each form when portraying particular events. This initial DA was used to generate profiles of each learner that in turn informed an instructional program focused on the tense–aspect system. The program was organized according to C-BLI principles but was tailored to individual learners based on their reciprocity to mediation. For example, some learners required practice on the formation of the *passé composé* and *imparfait*, including irregular forms, others were introduced immediately to the concept of verbal aspect, and still others required instruction on the inadequacy of previously learned rules for aspect use. Following approximately six weeks of instruction, a parallel version of the initial DA was administered along with a near transfer task depicting more complex events and a far transfer task for which the prompt was a written excerpt from a French literary text.

Analysis of video recordings of mediator–learner interactions documented the implicit-to-explicit organization of mediation employed along with a variety of learner reciprocating behaviors (Poehner, 2005). These are reproduced in Table 2.

Poehner was able to trace across interactions how much mediational support was needed to resolve particular kinds of problems. Note that the forms of learner reciprocity (right-hand column in the table) do not neatly parallel the mediational hierarchy. Arguably, some of these moves represent greater effort on the part of learners to assume responsibility for completing assessment tasks, but this is not straightforward. For instance, one learner might make a guess and then turn to the mediator for approval, while another might reject an offer of mediation resulting in failure to overcome the problem. Rather than higher or lower reciprocity, these might best be understood, as categories of learner engagement in DA that can provide additional insight into their ripening abilities (see Van der Aalsvoort & Lidz, 2002).

Another early L2 DA study greatly extended how learner reciprocity can be understood. Ableeva (2010) administered a DA with learners of L2 French focused on listening comprehension, an especially difficult feature of the language owing in part to the complexities of French phonology. In one-to-one sessions, the mediator listened alongside students to authentic French video

Table 2 A typology of mediation and learner reciprocity
(adapted from Poehner, 2005)

Mediation	Learner reciprocity
1. Helping move the narration along	1. Unresponsive
2. Accepting a learner's response	2. Repeating after the mediator
3. Request for repetition of learner response	3. Responding incorrectly
4. Request for verification of learner response	4. Request for additional assistance
5. Reminder of task directions	5. Incorporating feedback from mediator
6. Request for attempt at renarration	6. Overcoming a problem
7. Identifying specific site of problem/ error	7. Offering an explanation of thinking/reasoning
8. Specifying problem/error	8. Using mediator as a resource
9. Providing metalinguistic clue	9. Rejecting mediator's assistance
10. Offer translation	10. Negotiating mediation
11. Providing example or illustration of concept/principle	11. Creating opportunities to develop
12. Offering a choice between alternatives	12. Seeking mediator approval
13. Providing a correct response	
14. Providing explanation of correct response	
15. Asking for explanation from learner	

texts and offered prompts and leading questions to ascertain where comprehension problems occurred, including not only phonology but also knowledge of vocabulary, grammar, and culture. Ableeva's (2010) participants produced categories of reciprocity similar to those in Poehner's (2005) study, and she reported an additional category, imitating the mediator. This is noteworthy because it recalls Vygotsky's (2012) argument that imitation is a driver of development. However, he understood imitation not as simple copying or mimicry but as a phenomenon in which a person understands the intentions of the model, that is, the meaning behind each action. For instance, a person with no knowledge of music will perceive a conductor as moving hands about and looking randomly to different sections of an orchestra. Such a person would be able only to emulate but not imitate the conductor because imitation, in Vygotsky's sense, requires understanding how every stroke of the baton communicates important meanings to the musicians. *Imitating the mediator* in Ableeva's (2010) project referred to learner efforts to regulate their comprehension of the video texts, often by repeating the mediator's utterances.

According to Ableeva (2010), learner efforts to revise their comprehension of the texts in response to specific forms of mediation could be classified as *progressive* or *regressive*, thus revealing whether or not the revision displayed improvement in comprehension. Progressive moves include making a correct choice, deciphering a pattern or word correctly, and overcoming a problem, while regressive moves concern failure to make corrections, as when a learner switches from one incorrect response to another. Distinguishing progressive and regressive moves contextualized not only the number of mediating moves individual learners required to work through difficulties but also the effect of each form of mediation on learner performance. This information also revealed that some forms of mediation proved to be particularly useful for certain individuals, which was considered in preparing subsequent instruction.

3.4.2 L2 Group DA (G-DA)

In Vygotsky's discussions of the ZPD, he characterized it as involving dyads comprised of a child and an adult or a student and teacher. However, recall that he described the ZPD as important for identifying abilities that are still emerging and may be most easily guided by teaching. By grouping learners according to their ZPD, instruction can more effectively target those abilities and promote the development of each member of the group. With regard to assessment, is it similarly possible to introduce tasks that are beyond the present abilities of all learners in a group and to provide mediation to monitor the group's responsiveness? In other words, can the same principles that guide one-to-one DA be followed for procedures with a group of learners? If so, DA would be much more feasible in contexts where teachers are responsible for dozens of students and may not have the time and resources to engage with individual students for extended periods of time. Exploring this possibility is the goal of group DA (G-DA).

To our knowledge, the first extension of DA to an intact L2 classroom was reported by Poehner (2009). Tracy (pseudonym) was an experienced L2 Spanish instructor who designed her own primary school curriculum implemented in fifteen-minute daily lessons. She had become interested in DA after participating in professional development workshops and regarded it as a way to systematize her classroom-based assessment practices in order to track learner progress over time. This was especially important given the large number of students she worked with daily over a short time span. Tracy was concerned that in using interactionist DA, which she found attractive, it would be difficult to keep track of mediation as she engaged with full classes of young children. She therefore opted to use an interventionist approach, scripting in advance of each lesson a set of eight mediating prompts arranged from implicit to explicit. An example of these prompts is reproduced in Table 3.

Tracy sought to optimize students' engagement with Spanish during their fifteen-minute mini-lessons, and thus frequently made use of games involving the entire class (Poehner, 2009). This approach allowed all students to potentially benefit from the mediation provided to individual students. For instance, using the prompts from Table 3, she responded to learners who had difficulties marking Spanish noun-adjective concord. While Tracy's mediation supported an individual learner, other learners were able to observe the mediational process. Thus, when it was their turn to respond in a game, they were not necessarily beginning at the same point as previous learners had been because they had vicariously worked through the process of selecting adjective forms and observing Tracy's guidance. Poehner (2009) illustrates this with a sequence of learners who each took a turn playing a game that required them to describe an indigenous Peruvian animal. The first player required the most extensive support from Tracy, only completing the task when offered a choice of forms (the sixth mediating move from Table 3). Subsequent players required only the third mediating move and ultimately one learner required no support at all. Viewed collectively, Tracy was simultaneously mediating each learner's understanding of Spanish noun-adjective agreement even though she interacted with individual students.

A different approach to G-DA was explored by Poehner, Infante, and Takamiya (2018) in an advanced undergraduate L2 Japanese writing course. The instructor, Sayuri (pseudonym), was a native speaker of Japanese and an experienced teacher, who became interested in DA after participating in a professional development workshop. Sayuri reorganized the process approach

Table 3 A set of mediating prompts for classroom-based DA (adapted from Poehner, 2009)

1. Pause.
2. Repeat the whole phrase questioningly.
3. Repeat just the part of the sentence with the error.
4. Teacher asks, "What is wrong with that sentence?"
5. Teacher points out the incorrect word.
6. Teacher asks either/or question (*negros o negras?*).
7. Teacher identifies the correct answer.
8. Teacher explains why.

to writing and revision that she had previously used after learning about the ZPD and DA. Previously, she had relied on several procedures, including one-on-one sessions outside of class to review student drafts and offer feedback, in-class peer review of student texts, and a whole-class lesson on grammar topics appropriate for advanced learners but that did not specifically address struggles the class was experiencing.

Each activity was re-conceived as an opportunity for mediation attuned to learner emerging abilities. The one-on-one session was replaced by an individualized DA session in which she still reviewed student drafts, but instead of explicit corrections, she used graduated prompts, noting the language features that proved difficult for individual learners as well as how much support they required to identify errors. She used this information to place students in groups according to common struggles. Class time previously reserved for peer review was dedicated to small group work. Each group received a tailored packet of short texts containing the error types observed during Sayuri's mediation in the individualized sessions. The groups worked together to support one another and to collectively revise the errors they identified. Sayuri circulated among the groups to offer additional mediation as needed. Finally, rather than following a predetermined syllabus of advanced grammar topics, whole-class instruction was devoted to those errors that appeared most common in students' writing as well as errors that involved complex topics that Sayuri believed required explicit and detailed presentation.

According to Poehner, Infante, and Takamiya (2018), the teacher reported that the new DA-informed approach to writing revision enabled her to track learner progress toward targets that she identified for them as individuals even though much of the mediation was focused on the class. The G-DA was successful in supporting teacher and student interaction. At the same time, it is also the case that this was not a context in which assessment results needed to be reported to an external authority for purposes of high-stakes decision-making. In such a situation, there would no doubt be increased attention to generating scores or ratings for individual learners, and this approach to G-DA would perhaps require some degree of standardization of certain activities or procedures. As discussed earlier regarding *interventionist* and *interactionist* DA, the advantage for ease of comparison that is afforded by standardizing procedures generally comes at the cost of limiting mediator flexibility and, consequently, the potential to diagnose individual learner development. Balancing these interests is something that anyone pursuing DA must consider, taking account of the goals of the procedure and features of the context.

3.4.3 L2 Computerized DA (C-DA)

The question of whether DA might be efficiently undertaken with large numbers of learners has also led to efforts to computerize mediation in assessment contexts. Among the earliest discussions of computerized DA, or C-DA, were proposals by Jacobs (2001) and Guthke and Beckmann (2000). An important feature of both is that the assessment is paused when learners produce errors and is only resumed after brief instruction addressing the problem. In this way, the approach to mediation, while standardized, nonetheless embeds opportunities for teaching that includes tracking when learners require intervention and how effective it is in improving performance on the remainder of the test.

Jacob's (2001) C-DA model focused specifically on language aptitude among preschool-and school-aged children. The procedure began with videos of puppets introducing vocabulary and morphological patterns of an invented language based on Swahili. Children responded to a series of questions that assessed their ability to infer word meanings and to appropriately inflect words based on what they had learned from the video. When a learner failed to correctly answer a question, the computer program replayed the part of the video in which the relevant information was presented, and the learner was again presented with the question and permitted to formulate another response. If the second attempt was unsuccessful, the same video excerpt was replayed and a third attempt was permitted. If the learner was still unable to correctly respond, the program skipped to the next question. Outcomes of the assessment included the number of attempts learners made for each item, which the researchers interpreted as revealing the extent of their understanding of particular features of the language.

Guthke and Beckmann's (2000) C-DA approach offered an extension of the *Leipzig Lerntest*, a form of DA Guthke pioneered and employed with learners of various ages and that targeted a range of abilities. While we are unaware of any publication documenting the empirical results of their C-DA work, the authors' description of how the system functioned is worth considering. The C-DA was designed around constructs that were broken down into several dimensions with pairs of test items targeting each dimension. If learners answered one or both items in a pair incorrectly, the program paused the test and presented a brief instructional module that included an explanation of principles involved and a set of training tasks to practice using the principles. The test then resumed with another pair of items reflecting that same dimension of the focal construct. Guthke and Beckmann (2000) explained that this C-DA approach made it possible to identify both the underlying sources of learner difficulty (i.e., the dimensions of the construct that proved difficult for individuals) as well as whether those abilities were in a learner's ZPD as revealed by their post-instruction responses.

Both Jacobs' (2001) and Guthke and Beckmann's (2000) C-DA approaches entailed a single form of mediation, namely an instructional presentation, that could be made available to learners as needed. More recent efforts to design L2 C-DA have favored graduated mediational prompts in which a set of suggestions and hints are offered sequentially with the number of prompts learners require indicated in a final report. The first such project was Poehner and Lantolf's (2013) use of C-DA to diagnose reading and listening comprehension among university learners of Chinese, French, and Russian. Both reading and listening comprehension were further divided into sub-attributes that included knowledge of lexis, morphosyntax, and culture, with phonology added for listening comprehension. Written and aural texts like those commonly used in other standardized language tests were selected, and multiple-choice test items were designed to accompany the texts. Each item targeted at least one sub-attribute. The C-DA system in each of the three languages included a set of mediating prompts arranged from implicit to explicit for each test item. According to Poehner and Lantolf (2013), the multiple-choice format allowed learners repeated attempts to answer each question. When a learner's initial response was incorrect, the most implicit prompt was given and the learner was permitted a second attempt. This procedure continued until either the learner responded correctly or, if the learner's fourth attempt was unsuccessful, the correct response was revealed accompanied by an explanation. The reason for including an explanation of the solution was that it constituted an additional opportunity to mediate learner comprehension that could impact their performance on the remainder of the test. In fact, even when a learner selected a correct response, an explanation could still be accessed before moving to the next test item in the event the learner had guessed or was uncertain and wished to verify their reasoning.

A challenge that this C-DA program sought to address was how to represent the insights that the tests yielded regarding learner abilities, including their ZPD. A weighted scoring system was devised in which a *mediated score* was automatically calculated for each test item that ranged from four to zero points depending on the mediation needed by each examinee. At the end of the C-DA, a learner profile was generated that included: an overall mediated score; an overall *actual score* (assigning either the full four points for an item or no points); a breakdown of scores for items targeting the same sub-attribute; and a *learning potential score* or LPS. The LPS follows a proposal by Kozulin and Garb (2002) to calculate a single overall score that takes into account both a learner's independent performance (actual score) and ZPD (mediated score).

The formula for determining an LPS that Poehner and Lantolf (2013) adapted from Kozulin and Garb is LPS = (2 × mediated score − actual score)/maximum score.

While revisions to this formula have been recently proposed (see Sun, Xu, & Wang, 2023), the overall idea of situating the difference between the mediated and actual score in relation to the maximum possible score on the test has remained consistent. The convenience of producing a single score that initially motivated Kozulin and Garb (2002) to pursue an LPS, however, requires some caution. As Poehner and Lantolf (2013) explained, a more nuanced account of learner abilities, precise areas of difficulty they experience, and their ZPD requires information that is obscured if only one score is reported. It is for this reason that their C-DA program included LPS as one component of an overall learner profile.

Qin (2018) designed an interesting extension of this C-DA model in her work with university learners of L2 Chinese. The listening and reading comprehension constructs that were targeted in Poehner and Lantolf's (2013) approach meant that successfully responding to test items involved identifying details from the written or aural texts. Qin took this a step further by assessing learner comprehension of implicature, that is, not merely their understanding of an utterance but what pragmatic meaning is likely implied by the speaker. Qin's C-DA program included recordings of Chinese speakers responding to invitations, suggestions, and requests. In some cases, these were accepted by the speakers while in others they were refused, but how this act was accomplished varied greatly. For instance, a dialogue in which one speaker announces an impending visit to the city where the interlocutor resides and asks whether he could stay in her apartment is met with a response that the apartment is small and cramped. To successfully answer the test question, listeners must comprehend not only what is said but also its implicature. Consequently, the mediating prompts not only needed to draw learner attention to relevant portions of the aural text, they also needed to guide efforts to construct an accurate interpretation. The construct of implicature comprehension is complex, especially given that Chinese cultural norms differ from Western norms, and these differences became the focus of instructional intervention.

A third L2 C-DA model is Leontjev's (2016) ICAnDoIT system. Recognizing the potential for students to guess the correct response to a multiple-choice item, especially when each additional attempt reduces the degrees of freedom, Leontjev prepared sets of parallel test items for each construct to be assessed and permitted learners only a single attempt at each. If a learner selected the right option for the first item in the set, the message *Correct!* appeared, and the next item was presented. If, however, the learner answered incorrectly, an implicit mediating prompt was given before the second item appeared. If the learner answered this second item correctly, this was conveyed but if an incorrect response was selected a second, more explicit prompt was given. A total of five prompts for each set of test items was included in the ICAnDoIT system, and since no prompt was provided unless a learner made an incorrect choice, some learners completed the entire set of items without any prompts, while others required the full five. While Leontjev's C-DA model did not automatically calculate an LPS, the fact that each set of items was linked to a specific feature of English grammar (e.g., Wh- question formation) meant that by tracing the number of prompts learners received per set, it was evident which areas of grammar were most challenging for each individual.

3.5 Conclusion

The DA framework involves the systematic use of theoretical principles and concepts (e.g., mediation and ZPD), but it does not imply that a single procedure must be followed. Indeed, we have seen that various approaches and formats have been elaborated as researchers and practitioners employed DA with a range of populations and learner abilities. DA offers a valuable instantiation of praxis. Since Luria's (1961) introduction to the West of how Vygotsky understood the ZPD's importance, DA has stimulated considerable interest and innovation in educational contexts around the world. This work has resulted in attention to, and greater understanding of, phenomena including but not limited to learner engagement with mediation (*reciprocity*), recontextualization of emerging abilities (*transfer* and *transcendence*), and the ways in which mediated performance varies from independent performance (*learning potential*).

Since its introduction to the L2 field in the early 2000s, DA has been pursued with learners of a wide range of languages and at different proficiency levels, with procedures focusing on all aspects of language knowledge and ability. Poehner and Wang's (2021) time line of L2 DA publications included seventy-four published works, and this number continues to grow. Current trends in DA research include the possibilities for mediating learners that are presented through technological advances, interfaces between DA and other approaches to L2 assessment concerned with teaching and learning, and insights that are emerging as DA is taken up by researchers working in increasingly diverse contexts. Regarding this latter point, DA has attracted considerable attention in China, where the prevalence of high-stakes standardized tests and large class sizes offers a distinctive environment for trialing existing DA approaches and innovating new ones. A special issue of *The Modern Language Journal* in 2023 on SCT pedagogical research in East Asia included DA, and a 2023 special issue of *Language Assessment Quarterly* was devoted entirely to L2 DA research in China. As one example of the innovative nature of this work, Zhang (2023) implemented a five-stage DA model of listening assessment with middle school learners of English in China. The design included independent pre- and post-assessment as well as transfer assessments. A *targeted collaboration* phase employed eight graduated prompts that probed learner listening difficulties in specific areas including pronunciation, grammar, lexical knowledge, and use of listening strategies. Zhang included a control group that did not receive mediation. Comparisons of the performance of both groups' post-assessment and transfer assessments revealed that the DA group did better on the post-assessment and initial transfer but were not yet able to extend their development to more complex far transfer assessment. Such studies will certainly play an important role in the development of DA moving forward.

4 Teacher Education

4.1 Introduction

In Section 4, we consider two approaches to language teacher education that are firmly anchored in Vygotskian principles outlined in Section 1. Although each approach integrates the theoretical principles, each organizes its program in a different way. The first approach, referred to as the Barcelona Formative Model (BFM), developed by Olga Esteve and her colleagues at the University of Pompeu Fabra in Barcelona not only focuses on the development of individual teachers, but it has also had a significant impact on the language teaching programs in the Barcelona region of Spain (see Esteve et al., 2017). The second approach, Praxis-Oriented Pedagogy (PROP) has been constructed by Karen Johnson and her colleagues at the Pennsylvania State University and concentrates on the formation of novice language teachers without direct consideration of specific language programs. Each approach is comprised of several interconnected procedures and processes, and each has a substantial body of empirical evidence that demonstrates teacher development.

Both approaches adopt Vygotsky's key concept described with the Russian term *obuchenie*, which does not have an appropriate equivalent in English. Research on language pedagogy has devoted a good deal of discussion to whether or not classrooms should be teacher- or learner-centered with most researchers and educators today making the case for focus on learners. Much research has centered on the process through which learners develop L2 ability when they are not in a tutored setting on the assumption that if this can be determined classroom practice can be organized accordingly to maximize learner development. In our view, this approach is rooted in the belief that can be traced to the mid nineteenth-century thinking of philosophers and educators such as Herbert Spencer, who insisted that formal education would ensure success by introducing into the school context the procedures that children follow when they learn in the everyday world (Egan, 2002). Recall that for Vygotsky education is the artificial and systematic development of students and therefore should not adhere to the modes of learning that occur in everyday life. Consequently, his concern is not with learners or teachers, but with the dialectical social activity that transpires between them. Each component of this dialectical relationship is crucial to the overall success of the educational enterprise. This relationship Vygotsky captures through the concept of *obuchenie* – dialectical teaching–learning activity that promotes development (for a fuller discussion, see Nardo, 2021). BFM and PROP have integrated this key concept into their respective programs.

Vygotsky (1997a, p. 339) observed that failing to understand education as an activity focused on developing consciousness reduces the teacher to either "a simple pump" whose main responsibility is to fill students with knowledge or to what we might term "a personality" relying on charisma and a capacity to entertain students. To be sure, knowledge of the content area is essential, and establishing a rapport with students is indispensable. However, neither can substitute for a theoretical understanding of how developmental processes may be shaped through educational activity. An understanding of central concepts and principles is essential for guiding decision-making at all levels: curricular design, setting instructional goals and learning objectives, creating and adapting teaching materials, organizing classrooms, and facilitating interactions.

In our experience, many language teacher education programs do not provide opportunities to develop sophisticated understanding of a theory of development, SCT or otherwise. Instead, they offer overviews, at times superficial, of multiple and sometimes conflicting, theories. Consequently, teacher knowledge of theory does not provide an adequate basis to orient instruction and may simply offer a set of terms that teachers may or may not reference to explain their practices, which are likely shaped by their own experiences as language learners or by a model provided by other teachers. This situation parallels that described by Karpov (2003) in his discussion of Vygotskian concept-based instruction. Neither traditional teaching, with its emphasis on rote learning and mechanical practice, nor discovery approaches, in which learners are left to infer knowledge on their own, are likely to promote learner development (see Kirschner, Sweller, & Clark, 2006), and as a result learners rely upon whatever partial understanding they may have. Similarly, without a coherent theory of development to guide their practice, teachers may resort to what Lortie (1975) termed the *apprenticeship of observation*, a knowledge source derived from teachers' experiences as language students.

Although theory has generally not been emphasized in teacher education, this does not imply that it is irrelevant for teaching practice. Arguably, however, theories of SLA supported by basic research usually involving controlled experiments may not be optimal resources for teachers. Even though Vygotsky and his colleagues engaged in experimental research, he insisted that the true test of a theory is to be found in practice, including an educational practice in which teachers fulfill a dual role as practitioners and as researchers; in other words, practicing is researching. A monograph by Swain, Kinnear, and Steinman (2015) is a highly accessible explication of the central SCT concepts and principles, which are incorporated into both BFM and PROP. The monograph relies on real-life narratives to present the relevant theoretical knowledge and as such it can be a useful resource for those interested in exploring the practical implications of the theory, including those participating in BFM or PROP. The monograph, especially when used in conjunction with BFM and PROP can serve as a beneficial resource.

4.2 Setting the Stage

To set the stage for consideration of the two programs, we feel it important to address an issue that has been raised by VanPatten and two of his colleagues regarding SCT's focus on explicit instruction-learning that promotes development, the goal of BFM and PROP. VanPatten and Smith (2022, pp. 25–26) assert that SCT pedagogy "is concerned almost entirely with explicit learning" and "ignores implicit learning and implicit knowledge." We very much agree with this claim, and although we do not rule out the possibility that late learners can internalize some aspects of a new language implicitly, VanPatten and Smith (2022, p. 26) are mistaken in their contention that SCT focuses "on the kinds of rules and structures that classroom learners find in textbooks," including "things that fall outside of the typical concept of language, such as sarcasm." In our discussion of C-BLI, we showed that the kind of knowledge that is relevant for L2 development is nothing like traditional structure-based textbook rules. The concepts are meaning-based and are derived from Cognitive Linguistics, as well as SFL, powerful theories of language at odds with the structure-based theory proposed by Chomsky and adopted by VanPatten. Moreover, as Gibbs (1994) convincingly shows, figurative language, including sarcasm, constitutes an indispensable mode of human communication and can no longer be left out of the language curriculum.

We are not alone in insisting on the relevance of explicit instruction in a late-learned language. N. Ellis (2015), for instance, a leading figure in usage-based SLA, observes that "L2 acquisition by implicit means alone is limited in its success," especially when compared to L1 acquisition. According to Ellis, research confirms that despite years of exposure L2 learners often fail to detect language features that in the input either occur with low frequency (e.g., use of subjunctive mood in Spanish adjective clauses) or that in the speech stream are not very salient (e.g., English articles, usually produced with reduced volume and stress). Ellis (p. 13) also suggests that the attention patterns that late learners have developed through their L1 can block their ability to attend to L2 features and thus prevent input from becoming intake. He concludes that "learned attention limits the potential of implicit learning, and that is why explicit learning is *necessary* [italics added] in L2 acquisition" (p. 13).

There is evidence from neuroscience research that the brain system responsible for implicit learning, procedural memory, declines with age and therefore late learners are likely to increasingly rely on their declarative memory system, responsible for explicit learning beginning in early adult life. Indeed, Paradis (2009, p. 103) offers the following insightful commentary on the consequences of such a neurological transformation for late language learning:

> . . . if the aim of appropriation of a second language is to be able to communicate, and if one manages to do so with minimal use of automatic competence but with very efficient and speedy controlled metalinguistic knowledge the end justifies the means. The distinction between automatic [i.e., implicit] and speeded-up [i.e., explicit] is important as long as it is a theoretical question, but for practical purposes, successful L2 speakers do not mind how and by what means they are able to communicate, as long as they do so efficiently . . . for practical purposes, it does not really matter whether you use implicit memory or explicit knowledge. Who cares *how* you manage to pass for a native speaker of L2 ? As long as you are able to successfully communicate in the second language, and the more accurately and fluently the better, the question is moot.

While we do not believe it is necessary to communicate like a native speaker to be a successful user of a new language, we fully concur with Paradis's claim that success can emerge from explicitly internalized knowledge, provided that it is not the kind of knowledge expressed through traditional rules of thumb as assumed by VanPatten and others (e.g., DeKeyser, 2020; Ullman, 2020) to be the only way that explicit instruction can be implemented. Indeed, explicit knowledge may not play a "role in language acquisition as normally defined" (Lichtman & VanPatten, 2021, p. 298), which we assume is the model based on child acquisition, but it clearly can be the foundation of successful language learning as suggested by Paradis and supported by SCT-L2 research (see Lantolf, Xi, & Minakova, 2021).

4.3 Barcelona Formative Model (BFM)

The goal of the BFM is for teachers to appropriate three fundamental pedagogical concepts: conceptual understanding of language based on text genre rather than sentence as the unit of communication; focus on linguistic concepts "which infuse meaning into texts" rather than linguistic elements exemplified in sentences and explicated through traditional rules of thumb; and instructional sequence (rather than an instructional unit) that allow for linguistic concepts to emerge from "text-based communicative activities" and to be internalized by learners through "dialogic mediation" (Esteve, 2018, p. 490).

The BFM incorporates three phases designed to transform how teachers think about and engage learners in the classroom activity that is language development. To achieve this goal, it is essential for teachers to modify their pre-understanding as they proceed through the program. In other words, the OBA (see Section 2) that teachers bring into the program must change as they emerge from the program. To represent this change, we will use the following terms: pre-OBA (teachers' initial understanding of language and their teaching practices) and post-OBA (teachers' changed understanding of language and their teaching practices).

The initial phase of the program is designed for teachers to carry out a self-analysis of their pre-OBA relating to language, communication, assessment, learner development, grammar, grammatical exercises, communicative activities, and so forth. They are asked to respond to a series of questions relating to their understanding of grammar, its teaching and learning, communication, and what knowledge is necessary for learners to successfully participate in communicative events, assessment as evidence of language development, as well as what they consider to be core elements of language instruction (Esteve, 2018, p. 496). Teachers present their responses to their colleagues in the program for discussion and critique. They then produce what is called a "mind-map" showing how their responses are interconnected in their own thinking. The teacher educator provides the template for the mind-map (see Esteve, 2018, p. 496). In carrying out these two activities teachers often become aware of contradictions and inconsistencies in their pre-OBA. The mind-map is then brought back into focus a second time in the third phase of the program.

At the outset of the second phase, teachers are asked to engage in a dialogue with a colleague in their native language on a topic of common interest. The dialogue is recorded for collaborative analysis with regard to those features that teachers perceive as marking the dialogue as authentic or not. The teachers are then asked to decide if the classroom practices they use to promote learning are likely to lead learners to engage in authentic communicative interactions that share features with the dialogues the teachers generated themselves. They are asked to consider if and how they might change their practices to better enhance outcomes that empower learners to generate authentic communicative action. Teacher responses are then compared to what are called core-SCOBAs (Esteve, 2018, p. 496) designed by the teacher educator in consultation with a language researcher. Two of the SCOBAs depict a systematic and well-organized conceptualization of those features that mark a communicative event as authentic. Included here are such factors as presentation of self, speaker attitude toward a topic and an interlocutor (or reader in the case of written communication), appropriateness of vocabulary and grammatical elements, and the pragmatic function of the event. Teachers then express if their own understanding of communication is or is not reflected in the SCOBAs, if any of the concepts presented are surprising or puzzling, and if the SCOBAs suggest new ways of organizing their instruction to better enhance learner development (Esteve, 2018, p. 496). The third core SCOBA describes an instructional sequence that leads learners from a mediated analysis of a preselected text (oral or written) to an analysis of texts generated by the learners themselves. The focus of the analyses is on the concepts that reflect authentic communication. Teachers collaborate in responding to questions regarding the optimal point to introduce and explain the relevant concepts, appropriate ways of graphically representing the concepts as SCOBAs, and the activities necessary to mediate learner internalization of the concepts for effective communication (Esteve, 2018, p. 496). Teachers also comment on the difference between meaning-based linguistic concepts and traditional form-focused grammatical rules. Finally, they read and comment on several published C-BLI studies paying attention to the concepts in focus, the way in which the instructor organized a relevant conceptual explanation and how it was represented in a SCOBA, as well as the kinds of activities and assessment practices used in the study.

The third phase brings teachers back into contact with their pre-OBA, but before doing so, they develop an action plan comprised of a pedagogical proposal for instruction on a specific topic that incorporates the theoretical concepts considered in phase 2. The plan should address such questions as the following: which concepts are relevant?; what sources can be used to explicate the concepts?; what SCOBAs can most appropriately describe the concepts?; what specific actions need to be taken in class to implement the plan?; how does the proposal fits into the school curriculum?; what is the appropriate group of learners for the plan?; what will constitute evidence for the effectiveness of the plan and what instruments should be used to gather the evidence? (Esteve, 2018, p. 497). The plan is then implemented in the teacher's classroom. (Esteve, 2018, p. 497). Finally, each plan and the results of its implementation are brought into contact with each teacher's pre-OBA developed in phase 1. The purpose of this is to discover the extent to which their understanding of language and teaching have been transformed as a result of the BFM. They respond to such questions as how far have I moved on in relation to my point of departure? how did I become aware of changes in my thinking? what have been the crucial experiences that have resulted in my rethinking regarding my understanding of language and language teaching? how do I perceive my students and their relationship to me as a teacher? what insights have I gained through the conceptual work done? (Esteve, 2018, p. 497).

4.3.1 Reactions to BFM

In this subsection, we present the reactions of teachers and teacher educators who have experienced the BFM and who have implemented C-BLI in their own classrooms. The samples are drawn from Esteve (2018) and Lantolf and Esteve (2019).

Excerpt 1: experienced teacher

C-BI has led me to read some new theoretical books and to revisit handbooks on general linguistics and on the language I teach. It has also led me and my students to challenge well-established beliefs about the language we all are learning (for instance, that heavily colloquial language is easy to deal with) . . . I feel 'I am in process', like my own students. I experience a developmental process running parallel to theirs and find myself being surprised and/or learning alongside them . . . I believe learners gradually develop a more global view of language and become increasingly aware when they need to make appropriate adjustments. They have a deeper understanding of text genres and their features and are stepping into a less 'fragmented' dimension of the language they are learning. (Lantolf & Esteve, 2019, pp. 43–44)

The teacher is clearly rethinking, along with her students, about what language is in general and what the specific language in the teaching–learning experience is. She is willing to investigate what research has uncovered about the nature of language, which is an important transformative step away from traditional beliefs about pedagogical rules. She is learning something new about language along with her students, and they are moving away from a piecemeal understanding of language and toward a more coherent understanding based on language as genre.

Excerpt 2: experienced teacher

I feel my professional development as a teacher involves turning into a language researcher and providing my students with the best possible framework for them to become informed learners able to grasp and handle language as a structured whole. For me, such a framework is none other than C-BI [sic], as it clearly helps learners become language researchers as well through a translinguistic approach leading them to develop their plurilingual competence as a way to enhance their communicative competence (Lantolf & Esteve, 2019, p. 46).

Not only does this teacher engage in research as a means of improving her instructional practice, but because of their experience of language learning through C-BLI, her students also become researchers, not so much as engaging in formal research but to the extent that they explore the similarities and differences among the languages they know and are learning. Most students in the Barcelona regional schools are bilingual speakers of Spanish and Catalan and they also study at least one additional language in school.

Excerpt 3: novice teacher

In preparing classes and selecting texts to be worked on, I can address language complexity without leaving any aspect unconsidered ... Through CBI [sic], I can see beyond purely formal mistakes related to grammar or vocabulary and spot the students' creative use of language. This use accounts for their transformation process, i.e., for the extent to which they have gained control over the concepts dealt with, even if the linguistic elements used to express such concepts are not totally right (Esteve, 2018, p. 499).

This teacher clearly values creativity on the part of students, something that is central to Vygotsky's (2004) educational agenda. In this regard, recall the study by Yáñez-Prieto (2014) on promoting creative use of L2 Spanish. She also seems less concerned about selecting texts for her students because they might contain language features that they, or perhaps even she, had been unable to deal with.

Excerpt 4: teacher educator

The work with SCOBAs involves procedures that let emerge [sic] the teachers' own previous knowledge and professional experiences. It seems to naturally connect what is being learnt with each teacher's own background. This work represents a way, enjoyable for me and exciting for teachers, to ensure that information which might just have been merely transmitted gets actually transformed into knowledge ... (Esteve, 2018, p. 501).

Clearly for this teacher educator the outcome of the BFM has been very positive, not only in terms of motivation, but also in terms of how teachers think about language and how they are able to integrate conceptual knowledge into their instructional practices, as well as with regard to greater coherent and less idiosyncratic thinking across teachers as a group. The dialectical interaction between OBAs that teachers entered the program with (original pre-understanding) and

SCOBAs (depiction of theoretical knowledge) has resulted in a deeper understanding of language and its teaching.

4.4 Praxis-Oriented Pedagogy (PROP) in L2 Teacher Education

Over the past twenty years, Johnson and colleagues have employed SCT to inform their work in an MA TESOL program for novice teachers (e.g., Johnson, 2009; Johnson & Golombek, 2016, 2018; Johnson, Verity, & Childs, 2023). Just as many SCT scholars in the L2 field have shifted their orientation from interpreting to guiding development processes, Johnson and colleagues have elaborated what they term a PROP (our term), which they characterize as follows:

> a fundamental principle of VSCT [Vygotskian Sociocultural Theory] is to deploy specific VSCT principles and concepts to intentionally promote cognitive development through appropriately organized instructional practice, and to explore what that practice illuminates about our understanding of the principles we teach ... our work with novice L2 teachers over the past 30 years has changed how we understand Vygotsky's central principles and concepts. (Johnson, Verity, & Childs, 2023, pp. 15–16)

The program showcases an array of practices, such as careful selection of readings from the research literature, oral and written interactions with faculty members and practicing teachers who serve as mentors, classroom observations, and supervised teaching experiences. What distinguishes the program is how these experiences are theorized; that is, how they are organized for the purpose of mediating novice teachers' thinking about their activity and how it may ultimately promote learner language development.

Much of this work occurs in a sequence of three semester-long courses in which pedagogical concepts are introduced, their relevance to guiding teaching activity is modeled, and novice teachers are given opportunities to think with the concepts as they observe lessons, prepare their own instructional activities, engage in practice teaching, and reflect on these experiences through both written assignments and group discussions. These pedagogical concepts concern not the content of teaching but rather how teaching activity may be organized to support learner development. Thus, in contrast with the BFM, PROP does not include an explicit focus on how language curricula might be designed using linguistic concepts but rather its aim is "altering novice teachers' existing conceptual systems about language teachers/teaching ... by giving them new words, as well as new ways, for understanding and enacting the activity of language teaching" (Johnson, Verity, & Childs, 2023, p. 18). In particular, this new way of thinking about teaching is informed by what Johnson (2009) termed *teaching as dialogic mediation* in which classroom activities and interactions are approached as opportunities for intentional intervention in, and guiding of, learner language development. It is worth noting that students in the PROP program also take courses that explicitly and systematically analyze language use, and it is through those courses that they develop a conceptual understanding of language alongside the pedagogical concepts they engage with in the sequence of three semester-long courses designed by Johnson and colleagues.

The list of pedagogical concepts introduced in the PROP model is summarized in Table 4. Each concept is presented to learners as succinct axioms (the column on the left), which serve as reference points when the concepts are explained and modeled as the novices employ them to reflect on their own assumptions about language teaching and, later in the program, their own language teaching practice. As with the BFM, participants reflect on their assumptions, or pre-OBAs, regarding language teaching.

Several of the concepts aim to shift novice teachers from a more monologic discourse style (i.e., lecture) to one that creates opportunities for learners to express themselves and make connections, and for teachers and learners to be responsive to one another (e.g., ENGINEER PARTICIPATION; INSTRUCTIONAL PARAPHRASING; and TEACHING AS CONNECTING). Other concepts help to raise novice teachers' awareness of the importance of not assuming learners understand the intention behind lessons and activities or that they are necessarily prepared to engage in the class (e.g., ORIENT STUDENTS, PROVIDE RELEVANCE, and REASONING TEACHING). A particularly powerful pedagogical concept is BE DIRECT, NOT DIRECTIVE as it calls attention to *mediating* learner language use rather than *correcting* it. To be sure, there are occasions when explicit correction and metalinguistic explanation need to be the precise form of mediation learners require, but as explained in the discussion of DA, aligning mediation with learner responsiveness creates opportunities for learners to stretch their abilities and to actively identify, reflect on, and overcome difficulties in their language use.

As Johnson, Verity, and Childs (2023, p. 27) conclude, while these concepts "may appear simple," taken together "they actually represent a theoretical orientation to the activity of teaching that is built up through engagement in both theoretical understanding and practical activity, in short, through praxis." In the PROP program, instructors maintain a commitment to creating "structured mediational spaces where novice teachers are supported as they attempt to 'jump ahead of themselves'" (p. 20), while recognizing that achieving this requires careful alignment of mediation to individuals at each given moment. This alignment is possible only when the history of an individual is taken into account. Vygotsky's

Table 4 Pedagogical concepts in the PROP model of L2 teacher education (adapted from Johnson, Verity, & Childs, 2023)

Pedagogical concept	Explanation
ACTIVITY BUILDING	Instructional activities organized to progress in demands and complexity as learner abilities develop
BE DIRECT, NOT DIRECTIVE	Emphasizes learner engagement in language tasks without providing answers or completing tasks for them
CREATE PREDICTABILITY	Clarifying expectations for routines and activities, building coherence through transitions during lessons
EMBODIMENT IN TEACHING	Importance of body position, eye gaze, gesture, and physical presence in the classroom
ENGINEER PARTICIPATION	Communicate expectations for learner participation and create classroom environment that encourages participation
INSTRUCTIONAL PARAPHRASING	Acknowledge learner contributions and connect them to the lesson focus (repeat or recast utterances if necessary)
ORIENT STUDENTS	Explain coherence across activities and support students in identifying important features and making personal connections with content
PROVIDE RELEVANCE	Communicate lesson goals, purpose of activities, and expectations for what they should learn
REASONING TEACHING	Instructional choices reflect teacher goals and learning objectives, aiming to engage all learners
TEACHING AS CONNECTING	Building rapport and sense of community among learners; helping learners engage with content through variety of interactional opportunities

analysis of the role of the environment in development avoids mechanistic determinism through his emphasis on the refraction of environments through a person's history of lived experiences. Therefore, while the pedagogical concepts behind PROP do not vary, the regular dialogic interaction with novice teachers in the program is collaborative and dynamic. Indeed, the overarching focus on teaching as dialogic mediation is also expressed in the program through the dictum, TEACH OFF YOUR STUDENTS, NOT AT THEM.

To illustrate the kind of reorientation to language teaching that occurs among the novice teachers, Johnson, Verity, and Childs (2023) provide data that include: (1) recordings of actual teaching practices during tutoring sessions and a final teaching practicum experience, with attention to how these practices change over time; and (2) analysis of written reflections the students produce as journals, online posts, and course papers in order to trace their thinking about both the activity of language teaching and themselves as language teachers. In what follows, we present three excerpts from the novice teachers' written reflections that reveal their experiences developing a new way of theoretical reasoning about language teaching. All novice teachers were assigned pseudonyms. For additional examples and more detailed analysis, we refer readers to publications by Johnson and colleagues.

A common orientation to language teaching among novice teachers is to view themselves as the source of expertise and their responsibility as policing errors. A more nuanced view is proposed by the concept of mediation, and helping novice teachers to understand this invokes pedagogical concepts such as BE DIRECT, NOT DIRECTIVE and TEACHING AS CONNECTING. In the following excerpt, a novice teacher, Fen, described his experience of this shifting orientation during the tutoring internship:

> **I would feel anxious in my first several sessions with them** [the tutees] **because I was not sure about the "right" answers. But later I realized that it was not appropriate for me to give answers. What I should do was to use guidance to push them to think ... I began to ask more questions about their thoughts and reflections on her** [sic] **writing process and encouraged them to speak more in our tutoring meetings.** In this way I could know their expectations, their desires and how I could help them to achieve their goals. (Johnson, Verity, & Childs, 2023, p. 183, bold in original)

Rather than a more traditional, one-way form of interaction in which the tutor's task is "to give answers," Fen reoriented toward a *teaching as dialogic mediation* that relies upon guidance and questions to gain insights into learner thinking and to use that as the basis for his own contributions.

There is recurring emphasis throughout the program on working to build rapport with learners and to understand their backgrounds. This idea runs through many of the pedagogical concepts, and it is perhaps most explicit in TEACHING AS CONNECTING. Focusing not on errors that occur during a given activity but on learners as whole persons is, as mentioned, very much in line with Vygotsky's analysis of *perezhivanie* and the social situation of development. Taking account of the history of individual learners in order to more successfully guide their development – that is, TEACH OFF YOUR

STUDENTS, NOT AT THEM – is expressed succinctly in the final paper of another novice teacher (Aisha):

> I became more understanding than I already am, and **I found myself finding the importance and value of talking to a tutee as a person; knowing where they came from, what type of environment they grew up in, and their views on writing and so much more** . . . it can truly reveal to a different side of your tutee that may help you understand them and know the teaching method and learning style that suits them the best. (Johnson, Verity, & Childs, 2023, p. 189, bold in original)

These remarks from novice teachers in PROP, much like the reflections from teachers and teacher educators participating in the BFM, evidence the potential both have to bring about conceptual change in teacher understanding of language and language teaching. Such change, along with an understanding of the theory itself, provides a strong orientation for teachers to engage in *obuchenie*.

It is important to acknowledge that the kind of development that these programs pursue typically entails struggle on the part of teachers and teacher educators. One source of struggle is that those seeking to implement new practices often encounter constraints from school systems, particularly in the form of mandated curricula and materials and high-stakes tests. A common source of struggle for novice teachers, such as those who make up the majority of participants in PROP, involves anxiety over assuming the responsibilities of their new role as language teachers, which can be intensified if they are also endeavoring to follow a pedagogical approach that differs from that of their more seasoned colleagues. In the case of more experienced teachers, such as some of the BFM participants, they may need to negotiate the dissonance produced by this new way of thinking about language/language teaching with both their history as language learners and their years of teaching language.

Researchers have begun to document processes of teacher struggle as they navigate these difficulties in an attempt to implement SCT-informed pedagogies (e.g., Davin, Herazo, & Sagre, 2017; Williams et al., 2013). Van Compernolle and Henery (2015) report a case study documenting the efforts of one language teacher to adopt a Vygotskian concept-based approach to teaching the sociopragmatics of *tu-vous* in French. The teacher, Mrs. Hanks, was not only an experienced L2 educator but was also enrolled in a PhD program in SLA. Nevertheless, she required extensive mediation as she worked to understand uses of the second-person French pronouns *tu* and *vous* as features of a pragmatic conceptual system and how to present this information to learners. Mrs. Hanks collaborated with the researchers throughout the study to develop materials and activities and received their feedback on classroom interactions.

As the authors point out, the sustained support that Mrs. Hanks needed to successfully implement the program, despite her considerable teaching experience underscores the challenges inherent in provoking new orientations to language teaching. The authors further suggest that "short-term training sessions, which do not involve subsequent support from a more expert person, are likely to be ineffective in transforming teachers' pedagogical content knowledge, especially when this entails a radical re-conceptualization of language, language learning, and language teaching" (van Compernolle & Henery, 2015, p. 371). There is no doubt much to this observation. We would add that understanding SCT comes not simply from reading about it but from praxis, that is, from bringing the theory into practice and practice into theory, as occurs in BFM and PROP.

4.5 Conclusion

Sections 2 and 3 discussed, respectively, C-BLI and DA as approaches to L2 education that aspire to Vygotsky's vision of education as an activity that leads or guides psychological development. The success of such activities is directly dependent upon teachers. Many language teacher preparation programs that we are familiar with substitute language proficiency for language expertise and strive to provide a breadth of theoretical perspectives on teaching, learning, and development in the belief that teacher candidates can select concepts and principles according to their personal preferences. In our view, both of these practices are problematic. While proficiency in the target language is essential, it is not the same as the knowledge required to teach the language. Effective instruction relies upon conceptual understanding of the subject matter, in this case, language. Without systematic knowledge of linguistic concepts and how they are realized through particular features of the target language, teachers are likely to resort to rule of thumb explanations, which do not allow for the kind of knowledge necessary for learners to flexibly and creatively employ the language for communication. Similarly, becoming familiar with a variety of theories may be valuable for teacher candidates, but this will not enable them to gain the understanding of developmental processes that they will need to guide them as they select appropriate instructional materials, sequence lessons, design classroom activities, and so on.

In this section, we have presented two powerful approaches to language teacher education that take seriously Vygotsky's perspective that teachers are ultimately charged with organizing educational environments to support the development of all individuals. The BFM implements a concept-based instructional program intended to transform participants' thinking about language and language teaching. Their initial understanding, represented as a pre-orienting basis for action, serves as a necessary starting point to the program, while their post-orienting basis for action, which develops over the course of the program, represents the new understanding that will inform their future teaching practice. PROP seeks to move novice teachers' conceptualization of education away from models of monologic knowledge transmission and toward a view of *teaching as dialogic mediation*. This is pursued through carefully sequenced activities that guide participants' observations of, and reflections on, teaching practices, a process that is facilitated through the introduction of pedagogical concepts. The pedagogical concepts are presented as axiomatic expressions so as to be easily remembered, and each reflects a view of teaching and learner development that adheres to Vygotskian theory.

5 Concluding Remarks

A major challenge common to all areas of education is that teachers are likely to receive very different recommendations and guidance depending upon whom they consult and the theoretical tradition in which that individual works. In the case of language teaching, the situation is particularly complex because the field has not reached consensus on such matters as what precisely is being developed when learners study an L2, the status of L2 knowledge and abilities relative to L1, the extent to which cognitive processes in L2 development parallel those of L1 development, and what role formal instruction might play in guiding or facilitating developmental processes. As we have explained in this Element, SCT offers a coherent account of human consciousness and its development that is relevant for all domains of education. The four principles – *mediation, sociogenesis, internalization*, and *developmental stages* – outlined a century ago by Vygotsky – have provided researchers with a framework for understanding development of psychological abilities, including language, across the lifespan and in a variety of contexts, including formal learning environments. In the roughly forty years that L2 scholars have engaged with the theory, central concepts such as private speech and ZPD have generated numerous studies of the experiences of L2 teachers and learners, the quality of their interactions, and the consequences these have for learner developmental trajectories in the target language. As valuable as these insights have been, L2 SCT researchers over the past twenty years have increasingly shifted their efforts toward understanding developmental processes by actively promoting them through educational practices informed by the theory and relying on Vygotsky's genetic method. This refocusing of L2 SCT scholarship follows Vygotsky's own use of the four principles to guide research as well as his position that theory and research should not be regarded as a separate activity from practice but in a dialectical relationship with it. Specifically, theory and research provide the necessary orientation for practice, which in turn serves as a testing ground needed to refine and further elaborate theory, a relationship known as praxis (see Lantolf & Poehner, 2014).

Much L2 SCT praxis to date has been conducted as either C-BLI or DA. C-BLI emphasizes a presentation of the target language through linguistic concepts that constitute a type of explicit teaching, but one that differs qualitatively from traditional form-focused language instruction or rule-based approaches to teaching. The concepts in C-BLI draw learner attention to how particular features of the L2 are motivated by conceptual meaning, and in this way, they come to function as tools with which learners can regulate their language use, including in creative ways that may diverge from conventionalized norms. Activities are designed to promote learner internalization of the concepts, and a crucial feature of this process is the representation of the concepts in schematized form (SCOBAs). Mediation in DA is dialogic and follows an implicit-to-explicit sequencing, often in involving leading questions, hints, feedback, and modeling, for the purpose of expanding the scope of assessment to include both fully formed abilities and those that are still developing. DA follows Vygotsky's (2011) conviction that conventional assessments, which focus exclusively on learner independent performance of tasks and responses to questions, can only reveal abilities that have already completed their development; taking account of abilities that are continuing to "ripen" requires the integration of external mediation – through interaction – into the assessment procedure. The quality of mediation learners require, and their responsiveness to it (e.g., identifying problems with their performance, making appropriate corrections), indicates the effort that will likely be needed before learners are able to complete such tasks independently (Aljaafreh, 1992).

Both C-BLI and DA have generated considerable research literatures in the L2 field, highlights of which we have discussed in this Element. Collectively, this body of scholarship provides support for the position, which we believe SCT demands, that instructed SLA can entail much more than, for instance, the acquisition of a new lexicon for conveying existing (L1) meanings; rather, it involves the expansion of our semiotic resources, a deepening of our awareness and knowledge of language itself, and gaining control over a new system that may be creatively deployed for both communication and thinking. It is in this regard that the model of L2 education we have advocated throughout this Element is oriented fundamentally toward learner development, aligning with what Vygotsky referred to as *obuchenie*, or as teaching–learning activity that leads developmental processes. This vision for education is also ambitious because it proposes a fundamental rethinking of language and language teaching and assessment.

To that end, teacher education is vital. Both the BFM and PROP have yielded impressive results in transforming teacher thinking about the aims of language education and how they may be realized. These approaches help teachers develop expert theoretical knowledge of language, an understanding of developmental processes, and an orienting basis for how they can organize instructional environments and activities accordingly. In addition to formal programs such as these, we have, together and separately, led numerous workshops for language teachers around the world to introduce them to SCT principles and approaches such as C-BLI and DA. Often, external pressures influence teacher reactions, as when they report that assessments must be standardized and yield easily reported scores or that all interactions in the classroom must be conducted in the target language. Some of these responses reflect policies implemented by those with little knowledge of SLA or L2 education, and some no doubt are the result of multiple and competing accounts of SLA and the recommendations they provide to teachers. While a brief engagement with the theory is not likely to provoke changes to teacher thinking and practice, it is not uncommon that it provides a catalyst for more sustained inquiry and ultimately for researcher-teacher collaboration. Perhaps even, as has been documented in the BFM, teachers themselves, working at all educational levels, may become active researchers. We hope that this Element is sufficiently informative to stimulate teachers and teacher educators to delve even more deeply into the literature and to be daring enough to implement some of the ideas presented in this abbreviated introduction to the theory and its educational implications.

References

Ableeva, R. (2010). *Dynamic Assessment of Listening Comprehension in Second Language Learning*. Unpublished Doctoral Dissertation. University Park, PA: The Pennsylvania State University.

Aljaafreh, A. (1992). *Negative Feedback in Second Language Learning and the Zone of Proximal Development*. Newark, DE: University of Delaware.

Andersen, R. W. (1991). Development sequences: The emergence of aspect marking in second language acquisition. In T. Huebner & C. A. Ferguson, eds., *Second Language Acquisition and Linguistic Theories*. Amsterdam: John Benjamins, pp. 305–324.

Antón, M. (2003). Dynamic assessment of advanced foreign language learners. Paper presented at the annual meeting of the American Association for Applied Linguistics, Washington, DC.

Appel, G. & Lantolf, J. P. (1994). Speaking as mediation: A study of L1 and L2 text recall tasks. *The Modern Language Journal*, 78, 437–452.

Arievitch, I. M. (2017). *Beyond the Brain. An Agentive Activity Perspective on Mind, Development and Learning*. Rotterdam: Sense.

Baddeley, A. D. (2010). Working memory. *Current Biology*, 20, 136–140.

Brown, A. L. & Ferrara, R. A. (1985). Diagnosing zones of proximal development. In J. V. Wertsch, ed., *Culture, Communication, and Cognition: Vygotskian Perspectives*. New York: Cambridge University Press, pp. 273–305.

Budoff, M. (1968). Learning potential as a supplementary testing procedure. In J. Hellmuth, ed., *Learning Disorders. Vol. 3*. Seattle, WA: Special Child, pp. 295–343.

Budoff, M. & Friedman, M. (1964). "Learning potential" as an assessment approach to the adolescent mentally retarded. *Journal of Consulting Psychology*, 28, 434–439.

Campione, J. C., Brown, A. L., Ferrera, R. A., & Bryant, N. R. (1984). The zone of proximal development: Implications for individual differences and learning. In B. Rogoff & J. V. Wertsch, eds., *Children's Learning in the "Zone of Proximal Development."* San Francisco, CA: Jossy-Bass, pp. 77–92.

Danziger, K. (1997). *Naming the Mind. How Psychology Found Its Language.* Thousand Oaks, CA: Sage.

Davin, K. J., Herazo, J. D., & Sagre, A. (2017). Learning to mediate: Teacher appropriation of dynamic assessment. *Language Teaching Research*, 21, 632–651.

Davis, S., Ferholt, B., Clemson, H. G., Jansson, S.-M., & Marjanovic-Shane, A. (2015). *Dramatic Interaction in Education: Vygotskian and Sociocultural Approaches to Drama, Education and Research*. London: Bloomsbury.

DeKeyser, R. M. (2020). Skill acquisition theory. In B. VanPatten, G. D. Keating, & S. Wulff, eds., *Theories in Second Language Acquisition: An Introduction*. 3rd ed. New York: Routledge, pp. 83–104.

Dewaele, J.-M. & Moxsom-Turnbull, P. (2020). Visual cues and perception of emotional intensity among L1 and LX users of English. *International Journal of Multilingualism*, 17 (4), 499–515.

Di Pietro, R. J. (1987). *Strategic Interaction*. Cambridge: Cambridge University Press.

Egan, K. (2002). *Getting It Wrong from The Beginning: Our Progressivist Inheritance from Herbert Spencer, John Dewey, and Jean Piaget*. New Haven, CT: Yale University Press.

Ellis, N. (2015). Implicit and explicit language learning: Their dynamic interface and complexity. In P. Rebuschat, ed., *Implicit and Explicit Learning of Languages*. Amsterdam: John Benjamins, pp. 3–23.

Ellis, N. & Wulff, S. (2020). Usage-based approaches to L2 acquisition. In B. VanPatten, G. D. Keating, & S. Wulff, eds., *Theories in Second Language Acquisition. An Introduction*. New York: Routledge, pp. 63–82.

Engeness, I. (2021). *P. Y. Gal'perin's Development of Human Mental Activity: Lectures in Educational Psychology*. Cham: Springer.

Esteve, O. (2018). Concept-based instruction in teacher education programs in Spain as illustrated by the SCOBA-mediated Barcelona Formative Model. Helping teachers to become transformative practitioners. In J. P. Lantolf, M. E. Poehner, with M. Swain, eds., *The Routledge Handbook of Sociocultural Theory and Second Language Development*. New York: Routledge, pp. 487–504.

Esteve, O., Fernandez, F., Martin Peris, E., & Ateinza, E. (2017). The integrated plurilingual approach. A didactic model providing guidance to Spanish schools for reconceptualizing the teaching of additional languages. *Language and Sociocultural Theory*, 4 (1), 1–24.

Feuerstein, R., Rand, Y., & Hoffman, M. B. (1979). *The Dynamic Assessment of Retarded Performers: The Learning Potential Assessment Device, Theory, Instruments, and Techniques*. Baltimore, MD: University Park Press.

Feuerstein, R., Feuerstein, R. S., & Falik, L. H. (2015). *Beyond Smarter: Mediated Learning and the Brain's Capacity for Change*. New York: Teachers College Press.

Flavell, J. (1966). *La language privé. Bulletin de Psychologie*, 19, 698–701.

Frawley, W. & Lantolf, J. P. (1985). *L2 discourse. A Vygotskian perspective. Applied Linguistics*, 6, 19–44.

Gal'perin, P. I. (1968). Towards research of the intellectual development of the child. *International Journal of Psychology*, 3 (4), 257–271.

Gal'perin, P. Y. (1969). Stages in the development of mental acts. In M. Cole & I. Maltzman, eds., *A Handbook of Contemporary Soviet Psychology*. New York: Basic Books, pp. 249–276.

Gattegno, C. (1972). *Teaching Foreign Languages in Schools. The Silent Way. 2nd ed.* New York: Educational Solutions.

Gibbs, R. W., Jr. (1994). *The Poetics of Mind. Figurative Thought, Language, and Understanding*. New York: Cambridge University Press.

Guthke, J. & J. F. Beckmann. (2000). The learning test concept and its applications in practice. In C. S. Lidz & J. G. Elliott, eds., *Dynamic Assessment: Prevailing Models and Applications*. Amsterdam: Elsevier, pp. 17–69.

Haenen, J. (1996). *Piotr Gal'perin. Psychologist in Vygotsky's Footsteps*. Commack, NY: Nova Science.

Holodynski, M. (2013). The internalization theory of emotions: A cultural historical approach to the development of emotions. *Mind, Culture, and Activity*, 20 (1), 4–38.

Holzman, L. (2009). *Vygotsky at Work and Play*. New York: Routledge.

Jacobs, E. L. (2001). The effects of adding dynamic assessment components to a computerized preschool language screening test. *Communication Disorders Quarterly*, 22 (4), 217–226.

Johnson, K. E. (2009). *Second Language Teacher Education: A Sociocultural Perspective*. New York: Routledge.

Johnson, K. E. & Golombek, P. (2016). *Mindful L2 Teacher Education: A Sociocultural Perspective on Cultivating Teachers' Professional Development*. New York: Routledge.

Johnson, K. E. & Golombek, P. (2018). Making L2 teacher education matter through Vygotskian-inspired pedagogy and research. In J. P. Lantolf & M. E. Poehner with M. Swain, eds., *Routledge Handbook of Sociocultural Theory and Second Language Development*. New York: Routledge, pp. 443–456.

Johnson, K. E., Verity, D. P., & Childs, S. S. (2023). *Praxis-Oriented Pedagogy for Novice L2 Teachers. Developing Teacher Reasoning*. New York: Routledge.

Karpov, Y. V. (2003). Vygotsky's doctrine of scientific concepts: Its role for contemporary education. In A. Kozulin, B. Ginids, V. S. Ageyev, & S. M. Miller, eds., *Vygotsky's Educational Theory in Cultural Context*. Cambridge: Cambridge University Press, pp. 65–82.

Kirschner, P. A., Sweller, J., & Clark, R. E. (2006). Why minimal guidance during instruction does not work: Analysis of the failure of constructivist, discovery, problem-based, experiential, and inquiry-based teaching. *Educational Psychologist*, 41 (2), 75–86.

Kissling, E. (2023). Can concept-based language instruction change beginning learners' aspectual development? Preliminary experimental evidence that novice learners taught *boundedness* are less influenced by lexical aspect. *Journal of Applied Linguistics and Applied Literature: Dynamics and Advances*, 11(2) doi.org/10.22049/jalda.2023.27948.1447.

Kissling, E. & Muthusamy, T. (2022). Exploring boundedness for concept-based instruction of aspect: Evidence from learning the Spanish preterite and imperfect. *Modern Language Journal*, 106 (2), 371–392.

Kozulin, A. (2024). *The Cultural Mind. The Sociocultural Theory of Learning.* Cambridge: Cambridge University Press.

Kozulin, A. & Garb, E. (2002). Dynamic assessment of EFL text comprehension. *School Psychology International*, 23 (1), 112–127.

Krashen, S. D. (1982). *Principles and Practice in Second Language Acquisition.* Oxford: Pergamon Press.

Langacker, R. W. (2008). *Cognitive Grammar. A Basic Introduction.* Oxford: Oxford University Press.

Lantolf, J. P. & Poehner, M. E. (2004). Dynamic assessment of L2 development: Bringing the past into future. *Journal of Applied Linguistics*, 1 (1), 49–72.

Lantolf, J. P. & Beckett, T. (2009). Research timeline for sociocultural theory and second language acquisition. *Language Teaching*, 42, 459–475.

Lantolf, J. P. & Poehner, M. E. (2014). *Sociocultural Theory and the Pedagogical Imperative in L2 Education: Vygotskian Praxis and the Research/Practice Divide.* New York: Routledge.

Lantolf, J. P. & Zhang, X. (2017). Sociocultural theory and concept-based instruction. In S. Loewen & M. Sato, eds., *The Routledge Handbook of Instructed Second Language Acquisition.* New York: Routledge, pp. 146–165.

Lantolf, J. P. & Esteve, O. (2019). Concept-based instruction for concept-based instruction: A model for language teacher education. In M. Sato & S. Loewen, eds., *Evidence-Based Second Language Pedagogy. A Collection of Instructed Second Language Acquisition Studies.* New York: Routledge, pp. 27–51.

Lantolf, J. P., Xi, J., & Minakova, L. (2021). Research timeline for sociocultural theory: Concept-based language instruction (C-BLI). *Language Teaching*, 54 (3), 327–342.

Lee, H. (2012). *Concept-Based Approach to Second Language Teaching and Learning: Cognitive Linguistics-Inspired Instruction of English Phrasal Verbs.* Unpublished PhD Dissertation. University Park, PA: Pennsylvania State University.

Leontjev, D. (2016). *I Can Do It: The Impact of Computerised Adaptive Corrective Feedback on L2 English Learners.* Unpublished Doctoral Dissertation. Jyväskylä: The University of Jyväskylä.

Levitin, K. (1982). *One Is Not Born a Personality. A Biographical History of Soviet Psychology, Including "The Best Path to Man."* Kettering: Erythrós Press.

Lichtman, K. & VanPatten, B. (2021). Was Krashen right? Forty years later. *Foreign Language Annals*, 54, 283–305.

Lidz, C. S. (1991). *Practitioner's Guide to Dynamic Assessment*. New York: Guilford.

Lobman, C. & Lundquist, M. (2007). *Unscripted Learning. Using Improv Activities across the K-8 Curriculum*. New York: Teachers College Press.

Long, M. H. (1997). Construct validity in SLA research: A response to Firth and Wagner. *Modern Language Journal*, 81 (3), 318–323.

Lortie, D. (1975). *Schoolteacher: A Sociological Study*. Chicago, IL: University of Chicago Press.

Luria, A. R. (1961). Study of the abnormal child. *American Journal of Orthopsychiatry: A Journal of Human Behavior*, 31, 1–16.

Luria, A. R. (1973). *The Working Brain*. New York: Basic Books.

Luria, A. R. (1976). *Cognitive Development: Its Cultural and Social Foundations*. Cambridge, MA: Harvard University Press.

Nardo, A. (2021). Exploring a Vygotskian theory of education and its evolutionary foundations. *Educational Theory*, 71(3), 331–352.

Negueruela, E. (2003). *A Sociocultural Approach to the Teaching-Learning of Second Languages: Systemic-Theoretical Instruction and L2 Development*. Unpublished PhD Dissertation. . University Park, PA: Pennsylvania State University.

Paradis, M. (2009). *Declarative and Procedural Determinants of Second Languages*. Amsterdam: John Benjamins.

Pienemann, M. (1989). Is language teachable? Psycholinguistic experiments and hypotheses. *Applied Linguistics*, 10 (1), 52–79.

Pienemann, M. (1998). *Language Processing and Second Language Development. Processability Theory*. Amsterdam: John Benjamins.

Poehner, M. E. (2005). *Dynamic Assessment of Oral Proficiency Among Advanced L2 Learners of French*. Unpublished PhD dissertation. University Park, PA: The Pennsylvania State University.

Poehner, M. E. (2009). Group dynamic assessment: Mediation for the L2 classroom. *TESOL Quarterly*, 43 (3), 471–491.

Poehner, M. E. & Lantolf, J. P. (2013). Bringing the ZPD into the equation: Capturing L2 development during computerized dynamic assessment. *Language Teaching Research*, 17(3), 323–342.

Poehner, M. E., & van Compernolle, R. A. (2020). Reconsidering time and process in L2 Dynamic Assessment. In M. E. Poehner & O. Inbar-Lourie, eds., *Toward a Reconceptualization of L2 Classroom Assessment: Praxis and Researcher-Teacher Partnership*. Berlin: Springer, pp. 173–196.

Poehner, M. E. & Wang, Z. (2021). Dynamic assessment and second language development. *Language Teaching*, 54, 472–490.

Poehner, M. E., Infante, P., & Takamiya, Y. (2018). Mediation processes in support of learner L2 writing development: Individual, peer, and group contexts. *Journal of Cognitive Education and Psychology*, 17 (1), 112–132.

Qin, T. (2018). *Computerized Dynamic Assessment of L2 Chinese Implicature Comprehension*. Unpublished Doctoral Dissertation. Pittsburgh, PA: Carnegie Mellon University.

Ratner, C. (1990). *Vygotsky's Sociohistorical Psychology and Its Contemporary Applications*. New York: Plenum.

Sternberg, R. J. & Grigorenko, E. L. (2002). *Dynamic Testing: The Nature and Measurement of Learning Potential*. Cambridge: Cambridge University Press.

Sun, Z., Peng, X., & Wang, J. (2023). Dynamic Assessment of the learning potential of Chinese as a second language. *Language Assessment Quarterly*, 20 (1), 127–142.

Swain, M. (2006). Languaging, agency and collaboration in advanced language proficiency. In H. Byrnes, ed., *Advanced Language Learning: The Contribution of Halliday and Vygotsky*, Washington, DC: Georgetown University Press, pp. 95–108.

Swain, M., Kinnear, P., & Steinman, L. (2015). *Sociocultural Theory in Second Language Education. An Introduction Through Narratives*. *2nd ed.* Bristol: Multilingual Matters.

Talyzina, N. (1981). *The Psychology of Learning*. Moscow: Progress Press.

Ullman, M. T. (2020). The declarative/procedural model: A neurobiologically motivated theory of first and second language. In B. VanPatten, G. D. Keating, & S. Wulff, eds., *Theories in Second Language Acquisition. An Introduction*. *3rd ed*. New York: Routledge, pp. 128–161.

van Compernolle, R. A. (2012). *Developing Sociopragmatic Capacity in a Second Language through Concept-Based Instruction*. Unpublished PhD Dissertation. University Park, PA: Pennsylvania State University.

van Compernolle, R. A. (2014). *Sociocultural Theory and L2 Instructional Pragmatics*. Bristol: Multilingual Matters.

van Compernolle, R. A. & Henery, A. (2015). Learning to do concept-based pragmatics instruction: Teacher development and L2 pedagogical content knowledge. *Language Teaching Research*, 19 (3): 351–372.

Van der Aalsvoort, G. M. & Lidz, C. S. (2002). Reciprocity in dynamic assessment in classrooms: Taking contextual influences on individual learning into account. In G. M. Van der Aalsvoort, W. C. M. Resing, & A. J. J. M. Ruijssenaars, eds., *Learning Potential Assessment and Cognitive Training 7*. Amsterdam: Elsevier, pp. 111–144.

VanPatten, B. & Smith, M. (2022). *Explicit and Implicit Learning in Second Language Acquisition*. Cambridge: Cambridge University Press.

Veresov, N. (2010). Introducing cultural historical theory: Main concepts and principles of genetic research methodology. *Cultural-Historical Psychology*, 4, 83–90.

Verspoor, M. & Schmid, H-J. (2024). What counts as usage in dynamic usage-based models. In K. McManus, ed., *Usage in Second Language Acquisition: Critical Reflections for Theory and Research*. New York: Routledge, pp. 87–106.

Vocate, D. R. (1994). Self-talk and inner speech: Understanding the uniquely human aspects of intrapersonal communication. In D. R. Vocate, ed., *Intrapersonal Communication. Different Voices, Different Minds*. Hillsdale, NJ: Erlbaum, pp. 3–32.

Vygotsky, L. S. (1978). *Mind in Society. The Development of Higher Psychological Processes*. Cambridge, MA: Harvard University Press.

Vygotsky, L. S. (1986). Concrete human psychology. *Psikhologiya*, 1, 51–64.

Vygotsky, L. S. (1987). *The Collected Works of L. S. Vygotsky. Volume 1. Problems of General Psychology, Including the Volume Thinking and Speech*. New York: Plenum.

Vygotsky, L. S. (1993). *The Collected Works of L. S. Vygotsky. Volume 2. The Fundamentals of Defectology*. New York: Plenum.

Vygotsky, L. S. (1994). The problem of the environment. In R. van der Veer & J. Valsiner, *The Vygotsky Reader*. Oxford: Blackwell, pp. 338–354.

Vygotsky, L. S. (1997a). *Educational Psychology*. Boca Raton, FL: Nova Science.

Vygotsky, L. S. (1997b). *The Collected Works of L. S. Vygotsky. Volume 3. Problems of the Theory and History of Psychology*. New York: Plenum.

Vygotsky, L. S. (1997c). *The Collected Works of L. S. Vygotsky. Volume 4. The History of the Development of Higher Mental Functions*. New York: Plenum.

Vygotsky, L. S. (1998). *The Collected Works of L. S. Vygotsky. Volume 5. Child Psychology*. New York: Plenum.

Vygotsky, L. S. (2004). Imagination and creativity in childhood. *Journal of Russian and East European Psychology*, 42 (1), 7–97.

Vygotsky, L. S. (2011). The dynamics of the schoolchild's mental development in relation to teaching and learning. *Journal of Cognitive Education and Psychology*, 10, 198–211.

Vygotsky, L. S. (2012). *Thought and Language*. Cambridge, MA: MIT Press.

Wadsworth, B. J. (1984). *Piaget's Theory of Cognitive and Affective Development. 3rd ed.* New York: Longman.

Wertsch, J. V. (2007). Mediation. In H. Daniels, M. Cole, & J. V. Wertsch, eds., *The Cambridge Companion to Vygotsky.* New York: Cambridge University Press, pp. 178–192.

Williams, L., Abraham, L. B., & Negueruela-Azarola, E. (2013). Using concept-based instruction in the L2 classroom: Perspectives from current and future language teachers. *Language Teaching Research*, 17, 363–381.

Yáñez-Prieto, M.-del-C. (2014). Sense and subjectivity: Teaching literature from a sociocultural perspective. *Language and Sociocultural Theory*, 1 (2), 179–203.

Zhang, X. (2020). Testing the topic hypothesis: A concept-based teaching study. *Language and Sociocultural Theory*, 7 (2), 87–122.

Zhang, X. & Lantolf, J. P. (2015). Natural or artificial: Is the route of second language development teachable? *Language Learning*, 65 (1), 152–180.

Zhang, Y. (2023). Promoting young EFL learners' listening potential: A model of mediation in the framework of dynamic assessment. *The Modern Language Journal*, 107 (S1), 113–136.

Acknowledgments

This project was funded in part by a grant from the U.S. Department of Education to the Center for Advanced Language Proficiency Education and Research (CALPER) at The Pennsylvania State University (P229A180009). However, the contents do not necessarily represent the policy of the Department, and one should not assume endorsement by the Federal Government of the United States.

Cambridge Elements ≡

Language Teaching

Heath Rose
University of Oxford
Heath Rose is Professor of Applied Linguistics at the University of Oxford.
At Oxford, he is the course director of the MSc in Applied Linguistics for Language Teaching.
Before moving into academia, Heath worked as a language teacher in Australia
and Japan in both school and university contexts. He is author of numerous books, such as
Introducing Global Englishes, The Japanese Writing System, Data Collection Research
Methods in Applied Linguistics, and Global Englishes for Language Teaching. Heath's research
interests are firmly situated within the field of second language teaching, and
includes work on Global Englishes, teaching English as an international language, and
English Medium Instruction.

Jim McKinley
University College London
Jim McKinley is Professor of Applied Linguistics and TESOL at UCL, Institute
of Education, where he serves as Academic Head of Learning and Teaching. His major
research areas are second language writing in global contexts, the internationalisation of
higher education, and the relationship between teaching and research. Jim has edited or
authored numerous books, including the Routledge Handbook of Research
Methods in Applied Linguistics, Data Collection Research Methods in Applied Linguistics, and
Doing Research in Applied Linguistics. He is also an editor of the journal, System. Before
moving into academia, Jim taught in a range of diverse contexts including the US,
Australia, Japan and Uganda.

Advisory Board
Brian Paltridge, *University of Sydney*
Gary Barkhuizen, *University of Auckland*
Marta Gonzalez-Lloret, *University of Hawaii*
Li Wei, *UCL Institute of Education*
Victoria Murphy, *University of Oxford*
Diane Pecorari, *University of Leeds*
Christa Van der Walt, *Stellenbosch University*
Yongyan Zheng, *Fudan University*

About the Series
This Elements series aims to close the gap between researchers and practitioners by allying
research with language teaching practices, in its exploration of research-informed
teaching, and teaching-informed research. The series builds upon a rich history
of pedagogical research in its exploration of new insights within the field
of language teaching.

Cambridge Elements

Language Teaching

Elements in the Series

Printed in the United States
by Baker & Taylor Publisher Services